Let There Be Play

Bringing the Bible to Life with Young Children

By Jonathan Shmidt Chapman

Illustrated by Hector Borlasca

BEHRMAN HOUSE
www.behrmanhouse.com

www.applesandhoneypress.com

For Elior—who helped create this book as my
collaborator, my teacher, and my trusty sidekick.

For Sarah, Hadassah, and Susan z"l—
I stand on your shoulders.

———

Editorial Consultants: Debra Corman and Maxine Segal Handelman

Apples & Honey Press
An Imprint of Behrman House Publishers
Millburn, New Jersey 07041
www.applesandhoneypress.com
www.behrmanhouse.com

ISBN 978-1-68115-114-4

Quote on page 3 from *You Are Special: Neighborly Words of Wisdom from
Mister Rogers*, by Fred Rogers (New York: Penguin Books, 1995)

Library of Congress Catalog Number: 2023950203

Design by Tim Holtz
Edited by Dena Neusner and Deborah Bodin Cohen

Printed in China
9 8 7 6 5 4 3 2 1

Teach [these words] diligently to your children, and talk about them when you sit in your house, and when you walk by the way, and when you lie down, and when you rise up.

—Deuteronomy 11:19

Play is often talked about as if it were a relief from serious learning. But for children, play *is* serious learning. Play is really the work of childhood.

—Fred Rogers

Contents

DEUTERONOMY: FINDING OUR PLACE TO CALL HOME 167

Introduction

"Are you ready to cross the sea, Daddy?" said my four-year-old son, looking up at me.

There we stood in the middle of our messy living room, singing and dancing and giggling as we imagined that we were Israelites crossing the Sea of Reeds on our way out of Egypt. We had built our split "sea" from two bedsheets hung over chairs to create a tunnel. When we were done playing, my son looked up at me, his eyes wide and a big smile on his face. "Daddy, what happens next?" he asked. "When do we get to play the next part of the Torah story?"

When I became a parent, I started thinking about the ways we introduce Jewish tradition in early childhood (birth to seven years old). I had been working in professional theater for young audiences for over a decade, and I saw firsthand how imaginative play and creative learning could bring stories to life for children and families. I wondered: *What if these tools could be used to spark Jewish discovery, making it accessible and joyful for my son and other children?* This question began a journey that led me to create the book you now hold in your hands.

The author and his son Elior making clouds from cotton balls as part of an activity exploring the days of Creation.

Let There Be Play creates a playground out of the Torah (also known as the Five Books of Moses: Genesis, Exodus, Leviticus, Numbers, and Deuteronomy). The ancient text of the Torah is a centerpiece for Jewish communities, offering a platform for understanding tradition and helping us find meaning in our modern-day world. It is filled with the stories, lessons, and ideas that became the foundation of the Jewish people, and it holds meaning for other faith traditions as well. A section of the text, called a *parashah*, is read and studied each week in communities around the world. By the end of the yearlong cycle, on the holiday of Simchat Torah, we complete the whole Torah and start over again.

Despite the importance of this tradition for so many Jewish communities, we typically don't share the fullness of the Torah in early childhood. Sure, we may tell the story of Noah's ark or the Exodus from Egypt, but we don't get much further than that. What if we could use the whole Torah as a way to play, learn, and connect with young children?

In the fall of 2021, I launched an experiment to try to find something relevant and engaging to my then four-year-old in every section of the Torah and activate it through play. I know what you might be thinking . . . you can see this working with the easier stories of Genesis, but what about the much more challenging sections of the Bible, like the ones that focus on ritual sacrifice? What could my son possibly gain from exploring the ancient practices found in Leviticus? I made it my mission to dive deep into the entirety of the Torah to find at least one moment, story, or lesson in each weekly portion that he would find captivating and meaningful. It could have been a glorious failure of a pandemic-era project, but I was determined to try.

Each week for an entire year, I created activities for us to explore together at home, using the corresponding Torah story as a catalyst for artistic exploration. I also documented our experience and began to share the ideas with other families virtually. Our family Torah play became a highly anticipated weekly ritual that gave us the chance to learn about Jewish tradition while exploring big questions in our own lives. We were able to find something exciting and relevant to my son's life in each and every Torah section, including the ones in the middle that I previously thought needed to be avoided at all costs. We giggled, made a mess, and pretended to go on big adventures.

A Note about Creative Midrash

Creative interpretations of Torah are as old as Torah itself. Generations of scholars have played with the text in their own way, uncovering new meaning in the ancient words. We call this Midrash—a broad collection of stories, legends, explanations, and questions that attempt to fill in the gaps of the sparse biblical text. This book is designed to offer a new modern reinterpretation of the text, staying true to the original while providing a uniquely child-centered version of the stories, lessons, and ideas.

Telling a story from every section of the Torah that both honors the text *and* speaks directly to young children feels like walking a tightrope. We established a set of guiding principles to help us in the process. The stories have been carefully trimmed to focus on the parts most accessible to a young audience. The stories don't contradict the biblical text, but sometimes the emphasis differs to engage young children in a meaningful way. Creative dialogue and narrative details help make the stories relevant and purposeful for young readers. Perhaps these adapted stories will raise questions, ignite imagination, and begin an adventure with this ancient text that leads to further exploration and discovery.

Over time, my son learned about himself and his world through the ancient stories of our people. Lessons about kindness, sharing, compassion for others, caring for the natural world, and standing up for those who need help were brought to life through playing the stories of Rebecca, Jacob, Miriam, and Moses. My son became a part of the story, and it became part of him.

The experience also deeply impacted our relationship together. Once a week, I put my phone down and connected with him by being silly, asking big questions, and letting him take the lead. I became a better parent through playing with him. Imaginative and creative art making became a language for us to connect, learn, and grow together. My weekly engagement with the Bible text was surprisingly fruitful for me, too, as I made discoveries about myself as an individual, partner, and parent. I realized that by embodying the Torah through play, my son and I both found a way to feel *k'ilu*—"as if"—we were a part of the story ourselves.

And now, I invite you to use the activities we created in your own home, classroom, or community. Get ready to play, discover, learn, and invent together with the young children around you as you use the Bible as your art studio, maker lab, and theater stage. Whether you pick up an activity on a rainy day or follow along with the Torah portion as a weekly ritual, the act of playing the Bible together will spark joy and meaning for you and the children around you.

How to Use This Book

This book brings the Torah to life using creative play, imagination, and multisensory learning. It is designed for families at home, leaders of synagogue programs, and teachers in school to use with children ages four to seven. The stories have been adapted specifically for young children. The hands-on activities are easy to use and don't require any previous knowledge or extensive supplies.

You'll find the following sections throughout the chapters to guide you in discovering the stories of Jewish tradition, activating them through hands-on play, and connecting them to your lives today. You can choose to focus on one section or follow the whole arc of the chapter as you explore together:

 READ an age-appropriate and accessible telling of each Torah portion. This section is intended to be read aloud to children (or read by the child aloud if they are able), providing a catalyst to ignite curiosity and fuel active exploration.

 **IMAGINE** yourselves in the world of the story by asking questions that help children understand the lives of the biblical characters, the challenges they faced, and the choices they made.

 **MAKE** something that helps bring the story to life in a tactile way. These activities involve crafting and creating. Sometimes they involve cooking, cutting, and other steps that will need grown-up help. MAKE projects are often used as props in PLAY activities.

 EXPLORE through experimenting, building, and problem-solving. These STEM-based (science, technology, engineering, and math) activities bring the themes of the story to life through hands-on creative discovery.

 PLAY inside the world of the Torah using theater activities and imagination. Dress up, get into character, and bring the scene to life with easy-to-follow prompts to embody the stories through dramatic play.

Do you wonder about what these ancient stories can teach you and your children about your world? Spread throughout each chapter, you will find conversation starters in cloud shapes. These questions recognize personal experiences and strive to make meaning today through the world of the Torah.

Tips for Playing Bible Together

The activities in this book are designed for you and your child or group of children to experience together. They are created both for families to use at home and for educators to use in the classroom or community. You can explore a full chapter in one session or stretch out the sections over the course of a week or a few days.

Here are some tips to make the most of this book before you begin:

Decide where to start. There is one chapter for every week of the year, corresponding to the Torah reading cycle. You can start from the beginning of the book at your own pace or follow along with that week's Torah portion (beginning on or near the holiday of Simchat Torah).

Read through the chapter in advance, and gather the materials you'll need. Plan ahead so you feel ready to lead the activities. Most of the materials needed can be found around the house or classroom or easily sourced at the grocery store. You can also get creative and substitute different materials based on what you have.

Make time for a ritual of play. At home or in the classroom, set aside time each week to explore a chapter.

- **Parents and caregivers:** Try to create a weekly time without screens and other distractions, giving your child your undivided attention to learn and play together using this book as a tool. You can even create a special space in your home where you play these activities, and keep all the items you make together in that place.

- **Educators:** Create a weekly classroom ritual of exploring the Torah portion together through play. Designate a spot in your room that can be your Torah story location. Consider ways to extend the exploration beyond the classroom to your students' families at home (perhaps by providing follow-up questions).

Explore big questions together. The questions offered in the IMAGINE section and those appearing in the cloud frames don't have a "right" answer. They are intended to provoke curiosity and personal connection. Some of these questions have been debated by scholars for generations! Listen to the answers that your child provides, and share your thoughts with them too.

Jump in and play along. Don't be afraid to be silly, take on a role, and play along with your child. Many of the PLAY activities offer simple instructions for acting out a scene from the biblical story. Use these as a guide for your shared dramatic play. Your child will probably find it easier to dive into imaginative play than you will, so take their lead and let them be your guide.

- If you need warming up, try going to a mirror together and represent different emotions from the story with your facial expressions. Move your body into the shape of the character. How would they stand? How would they walk? Use these building-block activities to help you get into character.

- Practice the short lines provided in the PLAY activity instructions, or make up your own based on the scenario of the story.

- The PLAY activities usually include a role switch, so that each person gets a chance to play characters on both sides of a story. In this way, everyone has the opportunity to embody and understand different points of view.

Adapt play for a variety of ages. This book is designed for four- to seven-year-olds, activating the development milestones of pretend play, role taking, and symbolic thinking, while nurturing the capacity for understanding situations from multiple points of view. Adapt the activities based on the age of your child or classroom. With younger children, you can keep the activities short and guide them by modeling instructions first. For older children, use the questions to guide deeper exploration and allow them to take the lead on the activity with your support. Just as we read the Torah every year to learn something new, you can revisit these chapters over several years as your children get older and grow in their development.

Adapt the activities with a group of children. The activities are written in a simple and easy-to-use format, so that you can adapt them to suit your needs. For the MAKE activities, you can decide if each child should make the project or if you want to create one project for the whole group to complete together. Many of the PLAY activities offer a role-play in which two characters act out a scenario. You can choose to put the children in pairs and have them each take on one of the roles. Alternatively, you can ask a few volunteers to act out the scenario (and perhaps even add more characters from the story) while the rest of the group acts as the audience.

Adapting Activities for All Abilities and Learning Styles

The activities are designed to be enjoyed by any child, regardless of abilities or learning styles. That said, the activities can be adapted to meet a variety of needs. Here are some considerations that can help ensure that all children can engage in playing the Torah:

Find the style of participation that works best for your child or student. While each chapter is designed to be done as a full arc, you may find that certain section categories are more successful than others depending on the needs of the child. MAKE or PLAY activities might be ideal for a child who is sensory seeking, for example. The activities in these sections offer a range of multisensory engagement that may be ideal for a neurodivergent child. A more active, kinesthetic child may gravitate to the PLAY activities, while other children may enjoy the quiet focus of the MAKE activities or IMAGINE prompts. Feel free to emphasize certain sections of the chapters that feel particularly engaging to the child.

Create a visual schedule for the activity. For many children, having a road map to follow makes it more comfortable for them to participate. The framework of the chapters can also function as a schedule. You can share: "First we'll read a story, then we'll make something together, then we'll play a game, and finally we'll talk about what we learned." You can write or draw out the schedule and put it up on the wall, so that the child knows what is coming next.

Model the activity first. For some children, it will be helpful if you model the activity first and then invite them to join in. That way, they can observe the expectations and try it out when they feel comfortable.

Storytelling and role-play are powerful tools in teaching social interaction and connection. There are several role-play games included in the PLAY section. Research shows that role-play can be a powerful tool for children who struggle in social situations. They allow us to practice social interaction with a structured, known set of expectations. You can apply the strategies used in this book to other areas of the child's learning and development.

Lean into the child's interests to introduce and extend learning. Find out what your child is curious about, and use that as a bridge into the Bible play activities. For example, can you search online for images that correlate to the activities? Can you think about where dinosaurs fit into the story of Creation? Use your child's natural fascination and curiosity to fuel a connection to these activities, and follow their lead to extend the exploration.

Are You Ready to Play?

A Starting Ritual

Read this introduction aloud and act it out with your child to spark their curiosity and power on their imaginations before you begin.

Close your eyes.

Reach out your hands.

Imagine holding a very old scroll, a long paper with words on it, rolled up very tight. It is heavy in your arms.

Pretend to unroll it on three. One, two, three . . . open!

(Whisper:) Feel the parchment. It is rough and fragile. Be gentle.

This scroll is called the Torah.

It is filled with stories from a long, long, long time ago—but people all over the world still read the words written inside it every day.

Somewhere in the world there are people reading it right now.

Before it was even written down on a page, it was shared out loud as a story to imagine and remember.

It has been passed down from grown-ups to children for thousands of years.

And now it's your turn.

Listen closely. Do you hear them?
The characters are jumping off the page.
The stories are anxiously waiting to be told.
They want to meet *you*.

Are you ready to play together to bring them to life?

Open your eyes, turn on your imagination, and jump inside the Torah.

It's time. Here we go!

GENESIS
OUR STORY BEGINS

Follow the story of our world as it grows from a tiny spark into a busy planet. It all begins with the creation of light and darkness. Soon, living things fill every corner of the earth. They build families, embark on sprawling journeys, and learn about how to get along with each other.

You'll create the wonders of the world, join Abraham on an epic journey across the wilderness, help Rebecca feed some thirsty camels, and follow Joseph to the land of Egypt.

CHAPTER 1

Let There Be Everything

Genesis 1:1–6:8 • *Parashat B'reishit* • בְּרֵאשִׁית

Create something inspired by the days of Creation, name the animals, and think about the vastness of the universe as you take a rest.

Have you ever made something out of nothing?

Before everything was created, there was . . . nothing. It was very quiet and still.

At the very beginning, God created light. A radiant spark shone through the darkness. The next day, the sky was sculpted. Soon, the earth was formed, and oceans and rivers flowed across it. On the fourth day, the sun and the moon were hung in the sky, and stars blinked across the galaxy. Fish filled the seas, birds flew through the air, and every animal you can think of roamed the earth. Finally, on the sixth day, two humans were made. After creating everything, God took a very big rest.

Adam and Eve lived in a beautiful place called the Garden of Eden. They named all of the animals they saw.

"I will call you . . . elephant!" Adam said, looking up at a big gray thing with floppy ears and a long trunk. "And I will call you . . . zebra!" he said to the animal with black and white stripes.

Eve looked down at a long creature slithering at her feet. "And you . . . hmmm . . . you will be called . . . snake," she said.

God said they could eat the fruit from any tree they saw, except for one—the Tree of Knowledge, which stood tall in the middle of the garden. "*Hiss* . . . doesn't that apple look delicious?" the snake whispered to Eve one day.

She decided to take a bite and gave the apple to Adam too. Suddenly, they grew up. They knew that the world had both good and bad things, right and wrong. God said, "You didn't listen to Me. Now that you know more, you can't go back to before. You'll need to work like grown-ups, and you won't be able to stay and play in the garden all day."

Adam and Eve walked out of the garden, their eyes open to the vast and mysterious world around them.

Imagine Imagine yourself in the story of the creation of the whole world.

▶ Imagine a time before everything was created. What do you think it looked like?

▶ Why do you think light was created first? What would you create first?

▶ Why do you think Adam and Eve ate the fruit from the Tree of Knowledge even though they were told not to do it? What would you have done?

> What is something that doesn't yet exist in the world that you wish was created?

 Make Create clouds in your hands and pretend to float them across the sky.

▶ Hold a bunch of cotton balls clumped together in your hand, and pretend to float them above your head through the air like a cloud moving past.

▶ Now, attach them to a piece of construction paper using glue, creating a cloud shape of your choice.

▶ Look at all of the cloud shapes. What do they look like to you? Do they remind you of any animals or objects?

▶ Lay on your backs and hold your cloud creation above you. Slowly move it across your field of vision as if the cloud is moving past you in the sky.

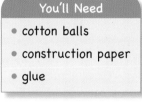

You'll Need
• cotton balls
• construction paper
• glue

Explore Create a leaf rubbing to discover the way leaves transport food and nutrients.

▶ Go outside and collect as many different kinds of leaves as possible.

▶ Put your favorite leaf under a piece of white paper.

▶ Take the wrapping off of a crayon. Turn the crayon on its side, and rub the crayon on the paper over the leaf.

▶ Notice the shape and texture of the leaf. Find the petiole, or stalk, that runs through the leaf giving it support, and the veins of the leaf that transport food and nutrients.

You'll Need
• leaves
• white paper
• crayons

Explore Become the earth and orbit around the sun.

▷ One person stands with the larger ball and plays the role of the sun. Another person stands a distance away with the smaller ball and plays the role of the earth. The earth "orbits" the sun in a circle, trying to keep the same distance as they go around.

▷ Explain that the earth orbits around the sun, and it takes a year to make this journey. How old are you? Orbit the sun that number of times. The children and the adults can each orbit, showing how many more rotations it takes as you get older!

> **You'll Need**
> - a small ball
> - a larger ball

> What do you think is the most incredible creation in the world? What about it makes it amazing?

For Groups:

With multiple players, you can incorporate the moon (orbiting around the person who plays the role of the earth) and other planets too. Try to make the whole solar system move together in orbit.

Play Play a game of creature charades to name animals like Adam and Eve did in the story.

▶ One person offers an environment: land, sea, or sky.

▶ The other person acts out the movement of a specific type of animal that inhabits that environment.

▶ The first person tries to guess the name of the creature.

▶ Now switch roles so that everyone has a turn offering the environment and acting out the animal.

▶ Pick one of the animals from the game. If you saw that animal before it was named, what name would you choose for it? Make up your own names for the animals you acted out in the game.

> Think about the snake in the story. What do you do when a friend tries to get you to do something you know you shouldn't do?

CHAPTER 2

Noah and the Very Big Flood

Genesis 6:9–11:32 • *Parashat No'ach* • נֹחַ

Create a tabletop storm, build an ark to protect your stuffed animals, and have a sunshine dance party.

Have you ever been caught in a really big storm?

One day, a farmer named Noah was feeding his animals when he heard the voice of God: "Noah, are you listening? A very big flood is coming! Water will soon cover the whole earth. Get ready now!"

Noah quickly ran home to tell his wife, Naamah, what he heard. "We've got to do something before the flood comes," Noah said.

He and Naamah built a very big boat called an ark to protect their family from the storm. They invited two of every animal to board the ark with them. As Noah was closing the ark's door, Naamah felt something wet fall onto her head. "Did you feel that?" she asked.

The drop became a drizzle, and the drizzle became a downpour. As the floodwaters covered everything in sight, Noah, Naamah, their family, and the animals were safe inside the ark. They floated on the water for forty days and forty nights.

When the rain finally stopped, Noah looked out of the windows of the ark and saw water in all directions. He sent a dove to check and see if any of the land was dry. The dove returned with an olive branch. "You know what this means?!" Noah jumped with joy. "Plants are growing again!"

As everybody walked out of the ark onto dry land, they squinted into the bright sunny sky and noticed something remarkable. The world's first rainbow stretched out above them—a reminder that after every storm comes beautiful light.

Imagine Imagine yourself boarding the ark as it starts to rain.

▶ Have you ever seen a really big storm? Was it scary? What did you do to feel safe?

▶ Can you imagine being in a boat with a lot of animals for forty days and nights? How would it feel? What would it smell like?

▶ What would you do to keep busy on the boat?

> What place in your life feels safe and cozy, like the inside of the ark in the story?

 Explore Make an ark out of small plastic building bricks, and send it off on the water into a storm.

▶ Use small plastic building bricks to create a small ark.

▶ Fill a large bowl or sink with water, and float the play ark you designed.

▶ Experiment with building and testing a variety of shapes to find one that most successfully floats along the water. (A symmetrical, balanced structure will float best!)

You'll Need
- plastic building bricks
- a large bowl filled with water
- a spray bottle

▶ Use a spray bottle and imagine it is the rain and wind of the storm. See if you can spray the mist to move the ark along the surface of the water. What else can you use to help move your ark along the water?

Play Build an ark for your animals!

▶ Spread blankets across two chairs, and put pillows on the floor in between to construct an ark that you can sit inside. With a group, add more chairs and pillows to create an ark that can fit everyone.

▶ Choose the stuffed animals who will join you on your journey, and bring them into your ark with you.

▶ Imagine that the rain has just begun to fall. What can you say to the stuffed animals to make them feel safe?

▶ Imagine the wind rocking the ark back and forth. Act out the movements of the ark by moving side to side together.

▶ The rain has stopped. Send a stuffed animal outside to see if the land is dry. Is it time to leave the ark?

▶ It's time to celebrate! Have a sunshine dance party. Pick a sun-themed song and dance! (We recommend the Beatles' song "Here Comes the Sun.")

You'll Need
- blankets
- chairs
- pillows
- stuffed animals

> Who takes care of you? Who do you take care of? How do we take care of each other?

CHAPTER 3

Abraham and Sarah's New Adventure

Genesis 12:1–17:27 • *Parashat Lech L'cha* • לֶךְ-לְךָ

Design a map, pack a bag, and go on a big journey.

Where is the farthest place you've ever traveled away from home?

One night while sitting in his tent, a shepherd named Abraham looked at the sun setting behind the mountains in the distance. He was just about to say good night to all of his sheep, when he heard the voice of God. "Go forth!"

"Go . . . go where?" Abraham wondered.

"It's time for you to travel far away to a new land and start a new adventure." Abraham jumped up from his seat. This could have been a scary command, but Abraham trusted the voice.

"Go forth . . . okay!" he thought as he ran straight to his wife, Sarah, and told her what he'd heard.

"What do you think? Our family is here; this is our home," he said to Sarah, out of breath from all the excitement.

"Don't worry," Sarah said calmly. "It won't be easy to leave this place, but no matter where we go, as long as we're together, it will feel like home."

God promised Abraham and Sarah that the generations of their family would grow and grow and grow in their new home, filling the world with love, stories, and tradition. Abraham and Sarah agreed that it sounded like a wonderful adventure. Early the next morning, they packed up the tent, told the sheep it was time to go, and set off into the unknown.

They hiked across hot sand, waded through a rushing river, and climbed steep hills. "We're almost there. I can see it up ahead," Sarah said to Abraham, who was out of breath a few steps behind her. Finally, they reached the land of Canaan.

"This is it," said Abraham.

"We're home," Sarah said, smiling.

Imagine **Imagine yourself going on a big journey, farther than you've ever traveled before.**

▶ How would you feel if you heard a voice telling you to "go forth" on a big adventure?

▶ How do you think Abraham and Sarah prepared for a big journey into the unknown? What would you have packed for the journey?

> Have you ever taken a big trip or journey? What do you remember about it?

 Explore Go forth and follow directions!

▶ Make four signs, one for each cardinal direction, to put around the room. Write N for North, E for East, W for West, and S for South (you can also use different colors for children who are too young to recognize letters). Use a compass (or compass app) to place the signs in the correct locations around the room.

> **You'll Need**
> • crayons
> • four sheets of paper

▶ Practice by calling out a direction and walking to the corresponding sign.

▶ Decide on a secret destination without sharing it with the other person (for example, the door). Guide the other person from one point in the room to the destination by calling out instructions using the cardinal directions. (For example, take five steps north; now take two steps east).

▶ Alternatively, you can draw a simple map charting a winding course from an origin to the destination (for example, from one part of the room to another, or from one room to a different room). Give the map to someone else, and let them lead. See if they can find their way from the beginning to the end.

> What do you think it would be like to move from a familiar home to a place you don't know?

Play   Imagine Abraham and Sarah's journey through the wilderness.

> **You'll Need**
> - bedsheets
> - pillows
> - blankets

▶ Spread out a bedsheet to create the shape of a river. Use pillows and blankets to build a mountain. Use your imagination to create a few different terrains, using the various materials to represent sand, forest, or water. Together, build an imaginative journey course through the room, with a beginning and an end.

▶ Use your imagination to take a big journey through the different landscapes you made. Start at the beginning and pretend to navigate each terrain. For example, imagine that you are crossing a river as you walk across the bedsheet. Move your body as if you are wading through the water.

Where do you hope to travel one day? What do you hope to see there?

▶ Imagine climbing a mountain, walking through mud, and traveling across sand in the hot sun. Think about what it would feel like, and move your body as if you were navigating each of these different environments.

CHAPTER 4

The Welcoming Tent

Genesis 18:1–22:24 • *Parashat Vayeira* • וַיֵּרָא

**Build a beautiful tent, welcome some weary travelers,
and help them along their journey.**

Have you ever needed to rest in the shade to hide from the hot sun?

At the end of a very hot day, Sarah rested inside the family tent to hide from the sweltering sun. Just as she was getting ready to take a nap, she heard the tired footsteps of travelers walking by.

"Excuse me . . . do you need a place to rest?" she heard Abraham call out to them.

Although exhausted from the day's heat, Abraham and Sarah didn't want to pass up the chance to be welcoming to fellow travelers. They poured the three guests some fresh water, bathed their feet, and cooked them a delicious meal. They even gave them directions.

As the guests set off down the path, Sarah heard one of them say, "You will be blessed for being so generous to us and making us feel welcome. You will soon become parents!"

Sarah laughed out loud. "What?! No, no, no. Abraham and I are way too old for that now."

But the mysterious guests were right. Before the end of the year, Sarah and Abraham welcomed a son named Isaac into their family, and their tent grew bigger. As she held baby Isaac underneath the twinkling stars, Sarah remembered the three guests and filled the quiet night with her joyful laughter.

Imagine Imagine yourself sitting at the edge of Sarah and Abraham's tent in the hot sun.

▶ How do you think Abraham and Sarah felt after they helped the travelers?

▶ How do you think the mysterious travelers knew that Sarah and Abraham would have a baby?

▶ The name Isaac means "someone who laughs." Why do you think Sarah chose this name for her son?

> How can you welcome a new friend who visits your house or joins your classroom? What can you do to include them?

 Make Build your own welcoming tent.

▶ Use a bedsheet and four chairs to create a tent that is open on all four sides and welcoming to all, like Abraham and Sarah's, tying the bedsheet to the chairs at four corners.

▶ Put pillows and blankets inside the tent to make it cozy.

▶ Create and decorate a welcome sign to put in front of your tent.

You'll Need
- a bedsheet
- chairs
- pillows
- blankets
- paper
- markers or crayons

 Play Welcome a stranger to your tent.

▶ Play the roles of the welcomer and the traveler. Decide which role each person will take first.

▶ The welcomer can sit at the edge of the tent, imagining it is very hot outside. The traveler should walk by, holding a backpack, pretending to be on a journey.

> When have you helped someone even when it wasn't easy for you, either because it was hard or it took a lot of time? How did it make you feel?

You'll Need
- a backpack
- a chair
- a cup of water
- a towel
- a plastic container with warm water
- paper

▶ The welcomer should invite the traveler into the tent to rest and offer to take care of them. The welcomer can:

- Give up their chair, and help the traveler to get comfortable.

- Offer the traveler a cup of water.

- Provide a wet towel to the traveler.

- Fill a large plastic container with warm water. Use it to set up a footbath, and let the traveler take a break with their feet in the water.

- Fold a piece of paper into a fan, and move it back and forth to cool down the traveler.

▶ Switch roles so that everyone gets a chance to be both traveler and welcomer.

For Groups:

With multiple players, you can have half of the group play the welcomer and half of the group play the traveler. You can also start with two people acting out the scene while the rest of the group watches as the audience. Take turns playing each of the roles.

Have you ever been surprised when something unexpected happened? What did you do?

CHAPTER 5

Rebecca and the Thirsty Camels

Genesis 23:1–25:18 • *Parashat Chayei Sarah* • חַיֵּי שָׂרָה

Fill a water well with kindness, create a camel puppet, and act out the story of Rebecca.

What qualities do you look for in a friend?

Rebecca lived a quiet life in the town of Haran. Every day, she got up early, walked to the center of town, and drew water from the well. "One day, I'll leave this place and see more of the world!" she promised herself as she pulled up a heavy bucket of water.

Meanwhile, many miles away, Isaac dreamed of finding a partner to explore the world with him. "It's lonely here in my tent!" Isaac thought to himself.

Isaac's father, Abraham, asked his assistant, Eliezer, for help. "Can you go out and look for a good partner for Isaac?" Eliezer accepted the mission. As the sun rose, Eliezer left for his journey along with ten camels. He traveled for many days across the desert.

One morning, Rebecca saw Eliezer and ten very tired camels lying out in the hot sun. "Do you need help?" she called. "Water . . . please . . . ," Eliezer whispered. Rebecca sprang into action. She carried jug after jug of water for Eliezer and the camels to drink.

Rebecca invited them all back to her family's house and made a delicious dinner for everyone.

"Rebecca, you have shown us so much kindness, giving us food and water and a place to rest," Eliezer said. "Would you like to travel with us to meet my friend Isaac? I think you and he would really get along."

Rebecca also dreamed of finding a partner to explore with—just like Isaac. Her family didn't want her to leave, but she convinced them it was time for her to see more of the world. They gave her their blessing to go and helped her pack up for the trip. She kissed them all goodbye, climbed onto a camel, and left to find adventure beyond her watering well.

 **Imagine** Imagine yourself resting at the well, waiting for water in the hot sun next to the camels.

▶ How do you get water to drink? What would it be like to travel to a well and carry water back home?

▶ How do you think Eliezer and the camels felt when Rebecca decided to help them?

▶ Do you think you would make the same decision as Rebecca, to leave home in search of adventure? Why or why not?

 Make Make a well filled with kindness.

▶ Think about all of the qualities of a kind person or a good friend. Can you think of specific ways that people can show kindness?

You'll Need
● blue construction paper
● crayons
● scissors
● a deep container or bucket

▶ Take a piece of blue construction paper, and draw four water droplet shapes on it, large enough to draw or write on (each about four inches tall and wide).

▶ On each droplet shape, write or draw a quality or action of a kind friend. (For a child who doesn't yet write, ask them for an idea and write it for them, or decorate the droplet shapes by drawing pictures on them together.)

▶ Cut them out and put them inside a deep container or bucket, imagining that you are filling a well with water.

▶ Over the course of the week, collect examples of kindness qualities and add them to your well.

> How have you shown kindness to someone else when they needed help? What did you do?

Make   Make a camel sock puppet.

▶ Take one sock, and put it on your arm.

▶ Ball up the other sock, and tuck it inside the sock on your arm to create the camel's hump.

▶ Use a permanent or laundry marker to create two eyes on the face of the puppet on your hand.

▶ Make sure you can open and close the puppet's "mouth," using your thumb as the bottom of the mouth and the rest of your fingers as the top.

▶ What does the camel move like? What does it sound like? Can you make the camel act thirsty? Tired? Happy?

▶ Take turns using the puppet to bring the camel to life.

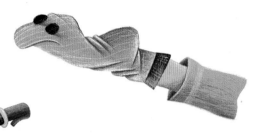

Play   Act out the story of Rebecca and the well, and show some kindness to a camel.

▶ Act out the story of Rebecca helping Eliezer and his camels. Decide who will play Rebecca and who will play Eliezer with his camel. (With a group of people playing, several people can create camel puppets, and Rebecca can take care of the whole group of camels).

You'll Need

- a well filled with kindness water droplets (from the MAKE activity)
- camel sock puppet (from the MAKE activity)
- a cup

▶ Rebecca sits in a spot near the well filled with kindness water droplets.

▶ Eliezer puts the camel puppet on and walks in, acting very tired and thirsty.

▶ Rebecca runs over to Eliezer and the camel and offers them water. Rebecca fills a cup with the kindness water droplets and offers it to the camel.

▶ The camel puppet drinks from the cup, and asks for more. Eliezer and the camel thank Rebecca for showing so much kindness to them!

▶ Once you've played this version, switch roles so that everyone gets a chance to play both roles.

> Is there somewhere in the world you've never been that you would like to visit? What do you want to see there?

> **TIP:** Practice using your face and your body to act out the feelings and actions of tired, hungry, helpful, and grateful.

CHAPTER 6

The Brothers and the Birthright

Genesis 25:19–28:9 • *Parashat Tol'dot* • תּוֹלְדוֹת

Dress up as Jacob or Esau, and act out their trade of a birthright for some stew.

Have you ever wanted something so badly you just couldn't wait?

Isaac and Rebecca got married and went on many adventures together. They became parents to twin sons, who were complete opposites. Jacob was quiet, organized, and liked to stay inside. Esau was wild, messy, and liked to be outdoors. Esau was born just a few moments before Jacob, so he got special older-brother privileges called a birthright. This made Jacob feel jealous. "Why does Esau get special privileges just because he's a little bit older?" Jacob wondered.

One day, Esau was tired and hungry after playing outside. He smelled something delicious. "Give me a bowl of the stew you are cooking!" Esau said.

"You can have my stew if you give me your birthright," Jacob replied.

Esau decided that his hunger was more important than his birthright . . . so he traded it for a bowl of stew!

When Isaac grew old and could barely see anymore, he called Esau to his tent. "Cook me my favorite meal, and I'll give you a blessing to lead our family," he said.

Rebecca overheard. Although she loved both her sons, she thought Isaac would make a better family leader. "Your dad is about to give Esau his blessing to lead our family," Rebecca whispered to Jacob. "That blessing should be yours. I'll help you get it." Rebecca cooked Isaac's favorite meal and put Jacob in Esau's fuzzy sweater, because Esau had much more hair on his arms than Jacob.

"Who is at the door with my favorite food?" Isaac asked. "It is your son, Esau," Jacob pretended. He put out his arm for Isaac to feel, tricking his dad into thinking he was his brother. Isaac ate the meal and gave Jacob his blessing to lead the family.

"Where are you, Jacob?!" Esau screamed when he realized what happened. "I can't believe you tricked me twice!!" Afraid of what Esau might do to him, Jacob quickly packed his bag and ran far away into the wilderness. He set off in the direction of his mother's home, near the well, hoping to find a welcoming place to rest.

Imagine Imagine yourself feeling so hungry that you give up your special privileges for a bowl of yummy stew.

▶ How would you have acted in Esau's place? What choice would you have made when you got home feeling really hungry? What would you have said to Jacob?

▶ How would you have acted in Jacob's place? Would you have tricked Isaac into giving you the blessing instead of Esau? Why or why not?

> How are you similar and different from the other people who live in your house?

 Make Design opposite looks for Jacob and Esau.

▶ Photocopy or trace the Jacob and Esau Template (page 36), and draw an outfit for Jacob and for Esau. Think about the colors you can use to bring them to life. How can you use your drawing to show Jacob as quiet and clean and Esau as wild and messy?

You'll Need
- Jacob and Esau Template (page 36)
- crayons
- various pieces of clothing

▶ Inspired by your drawings, create costumes for Jacob and Esau using various clothing pieces to dress up. Find pieces of clothing that best match the colors and shapes you drew.

▶ Try on your costume to get into character as Jacob or Esau.

▶ Alternatively, transform from Jacob to Esau. How can you change your facial expression, your body pose, and your clothes to go from organized to messy or from quiet to wild? Try changing back and forth between Jacob and Esau, showing these opposites with the way you look and move.

> Why do you think grown-ups ask kids to be patient?

Play **Act out the story of Esau giving away his birthright for a bowl of stew.**

> | You'll Need |
> | --- |
> | • toys to create a "stew" |
> | • a bowl |
> | • a spoon |
> | • paper |
> | • crayons |

▶ Create a "stew" out of toys. (For example, you can fill a bowl with blocks or alphabet magnets.)

▶ Write "Birthright" on a piece of paper, and decorate it.

▶ Decide who will play Jacob and who will play Esau.

▶ Jacob sits stirring the "stew" with the spoon. Esau comes in holding the birthright paper, acting very tired and hungry. Esau says, "Jacob, give me some of your stew!"

▶ Jacob says, "Let's make a trade: your birthright for a bowl of stew!"

▶ Esau thinks about this choice. How can you show with your face or your actions that he's trying to decide what to do? How do you think he feels?

▶ Esau exchanges the birthright for a bowl of stew. He "eats" it.

▶ Jacob takes the birthright. How can you show how he feels about making this trade with your face and your actions?

▶ Jacob runs away with the birthright, and Esau is very angry now that he realizes what he did!

▶ Once you've played this version, switch roles so that everyone gets a chance at playing both roles.

> How do you feel when you have to wait for a treat instead of getting it right away?

For Groups:

With multiple players, you can have half of the group play Jacob and half of the group play Esau. You can also start with two people acting out the scene while the rest of the group watches as the audience. Take turns playing each of the roles.

Jacob and Esau Template

Design outfits for Jacob and Esau for the MAKE activity on page 34.

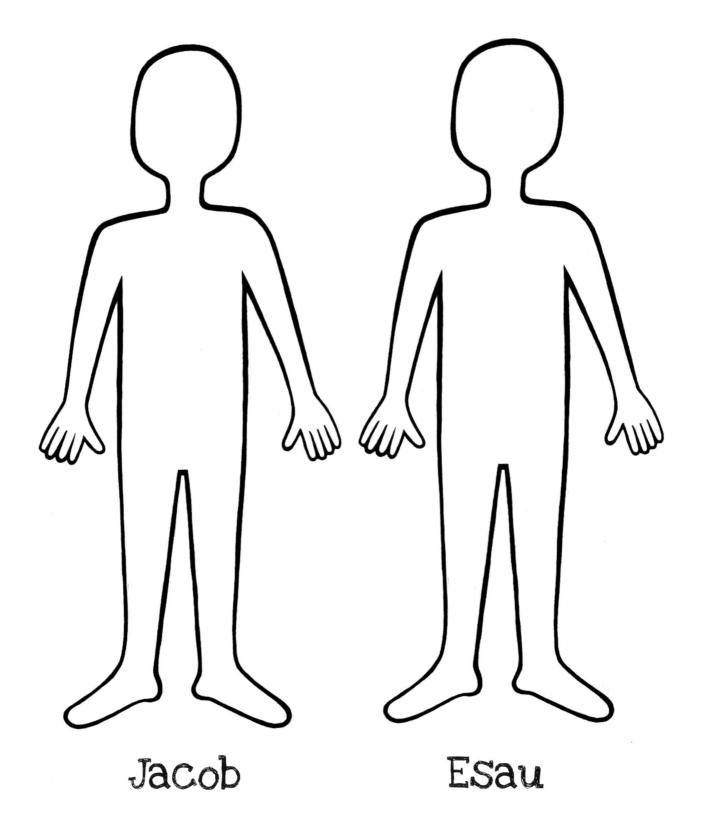

Jacob   Esau

CHAPTER 7

Jacob and the Ladder to the Sky

Genesis 28:10–32:3 • *Parashat Vayeitzei* • וַיֵּצֵא

Imagine a ladder going to the sky, play in the clouds, and bring Jacob's dream to life.

Have you ever had a dream that felt real?

"Just keep running," Jacob said to himself, out of breath. He ran far away from home, afraid of what his brother Esau might do to him for taking both his birthright and blessing. After traveling as far as his feet could take him, Jacob stopped to rest for the night in the wilderness.

"This looks like the perfect spot to lay down and rest," he thought to himself. He put stones around his head to protect him while he slept and fell fast asleep.

As soon as he closed his eyes, he began to dream. He dreamed that a ladder stretched from the ground where he slept all the way up to the sky, stretching beyond the clouds. As Jacob looked up, he saw angels traveling up and down the ladder. He heard God's voice saying, "I will be with you, and I will protect you wherever you go. You will not be alone, and your family will grow and grow to spread across the world."

When Jacob woke up, he didn't feel afraid anymore. "It's time for me to stop running and make a new home," he thought. He continued on his journey and finally arrived in Haran—the same city where his mother, Rebecca, grew up and where his grandparents, Sarah and Abraham, had lived. There he met two sisters named Rachel and Leah. Together they built a tent that could hold a very, very big family. Many years later, as he watched his thirteen children running around outside in the moonlight, Jacob suddenly remembered that dream he had in the wilderness. "It came true!" he said as he looked up at the stars in the sky and smiled.

Imagine Imagine yourself lying down to rest in the wilderness after traveling all day.

▶ How would you feel if you went to sleep in the wilderness far away from home?

▶ What do you think the view looked like from the bottom of the ladder in Jacob's dream?

▶ Try to interpret Jacob's dream. What do you think it meant?

> What do you dream about when you sleep?

 Make Set up Jacob's resting place and re-create his dream.

▶ Choose a space where you have room to spread out.

▶ Use masking tape to create the shape of a big ladder on your floor. Create two long lines of tape, and then create the rungs of the ladder across.

▶ At the "bottom" of the ladder, set up the place that Jacob slept. You can use blankets, and then put a circle of rocks around the blanket. (If you don't want to collect rocks, you can use blocks.)

You'll Need
- masking tape
- blankets
- rocks (or blocks)
- pillows
- bedsheets
- flashlights/colored lights

▶ At the "top" of the ladder, create the clouds in the sky. Lay pillows across the floor, and cover them with a bedsheet. You can use any special lights you have to make the space feel even more magical.

> Jacob's dream makes him feel better when he is scared. When you are feeling afraid, what makes you feel better?

Play Climb a ladder to the sky.

▶ Lay down in the circle of rocks at the "bottom" of the ladder. Close your eyes and pretend to sleep.

▶ When you are ready, wake up and find the ladder. "Climb" the ladder slowly, and find the sky at the top.

▶ Explore the clouds! Jump, roll, and snuggle in the pillows, imagining you are in the sky.

▶ One person can explore the clouds, while the other can deliver the message Jacob heard, saying aloud, "I will be with you. I will protect you wherever you go!"

▶ When you are ready, climb back down the ladder, and pretend to go back to sleep.

> **You'll Need**
> • the dream space you created (from the MAKE activity)

> Imagine falling asleep outside. What do you hear around you as you drift off to sleep?

CHAPTER 8

The Reunion of the Brothers

Genesis 32:4–36:43 • *Parashat Vayishlach* • וַיִּשְׁלַח

Build a miniature model of Jacob and Esau's reunion, and act out the moment they see each other again.

Have you ever apologized to a friend after having a fight?

Jacob couldn't sleep. His thirteen children were making so much noise! Their big tent was starting to feel small as the children grew up. "It's time for us to move," Jacob said. "Let's pack up and bring the family to Canaan."

Jacob was excited to go back home after all these years, but he was nervous to see his brother Esau again. "Will he still be mad at me for taking his birthright and getting his blessing when we were younger?" Jacob wondered. "I need to make things right."

He sent a message to Esau, and he waited. And waited. And waited. Would Esau agree to see him again? Finally, Esau sent a message in return. "Let's meet, brother," Esau wrote.

Jacob felt worried. The last time they were together, Esau was very angry at him. "What if he won't forgive me?" Jacob said to Rachel and Leah.

"Leah and I sometimes fight, but we always make up," said Rachel.

"No matter what happens or how mad you get at each other, family is family," Leah added.

The big day finally arrived. Jacob prepared a gift for his brother, hoping to show Esau he was sorry for everything that had happened. Jacob stood with his family and animals at his side. Esau also brought his whole family and all of his animals too. Jacob took a step forward. Then Esau took a step forward. They stopped and held their breath, waiting to see what the other would do. Finally, Jacob bowed down to the ground seven times. To Jacob's surprise, Esau ran to greet him, hugged him, and kissed him! The brothers were finally reunited.

Imagine Imagine yourself reuniting with your long-lost sibling after many, many years.

▶ How do you think the brothers felt when they saw each other for the first time in many years?

▶ Why do you think Jacob bowed down to the ground? What do you think he was trying to show Esau?

▶ Why do you think Esau decided to hug and kiss Jacob?

What are the steps you can take when apologizing to someone?

 Make Create a gift of apology.

▶ Think about the gift that Jacob gave to Esau as an apology. What could have been inside? What would you give to a friend to ask for their forgiveness? Do you think a gift is needed to show you are sorry?

▶ Draw a gift box on a piece of paper.

▶ Draw the best present you can think of to give to Esau inside of the box.

You'll Need
- paper
- crayons

 Make Make a miniature scene of the brothers' reunion.

▶ Imagine the reunion place where Jacob and Esau meet.

▶ Set up Jacob and Esau's camps facing each other, just before the reunion.

▶ Choose a doll, action figure, or small plastic model to represent Jacob. Set up all of Jacob's family, friends, and animals behind him, using other dolls or toys.

▶ Now, choose a doll, action figure, or small plastic model to represent Esau, standing across from Jacob at a distance. Set up all of Esau's family, friends, and animals behind him, using other dolls or toys.

You'll Need
- small plastic models, action figures, dolls, or other toys

How can you show someone that you forgive them?

▶ Imagine what each of these characters is thinking. You can hold each doll as you say their thoughts out loud.

Play

Become Jacob and Esau, and act out the moment when the brothers see each other again.

▶ Decide who will play Jacob and who will play Esau. Jacob and Esau stand a few feet away from each other, staring at each other.

▶ How do you think Jacob feels? Is he scared? Worried? The person playing Jacob can show the feeling using their face and body.

▶ How do you think Esau feels? Is he angry? Nervous? Excited? The person playing Esau can show the feeling using their face and body.

▶ Jacob walks toward Esau and hands him a present. Then, Jacob bows down to the floor seven times.

▶ Esau helps Jacob up from the floor and gives him a big hug!

▶ What do you think they say to each other? Add your own dialogue as you play. (An example might be: "It's so good to finally see you again, brother!")

> Think about a fight you've had with a sibling or friend. What was it about, and how did you make up?

▶ Now switch roles and act out the scene again.

For Groups:

With multiple players, you can have half of the group play Jacob and half of the group play Esau. You can also start with two people acting out the scene while the rest of the group watches as the audience. Take turns playing each of the roles.

CHAPTER 9

Joseph and His Wild Dreams

Genesis 37:1–40:23 • *Parashat Vayeishev* • וַיֵּשֶׁב

Create Joseph's rainbow coat, and perform a puppet show of dreams.

Have you ever been jealous of someone else?

Jacob had a big family, and their tent in Canaan buzzed with the sound of twelve sons and a daughter running around. Jacob couldn't hide the fact that Joseph was his favorite of all of his children. One day, Jacob gave Joseph a special present.

"Joseph, try on this beautiful coat decorated with many colors. It's one of a kind, just like you," Jacob said as he helped Joseph put it on.

All of Joseph's brothers were very jealous. "Why does he get a fancy coat? What's so special about him anyway?" they grumbled.

Joseph made them even angrier when he told them about his dreams. "You're not going to believe this," Joseph said to his family. "I had a wild dream that all of your bundles of wheat bowed down to my bundle, the biggest of all. And there's more. I also dreamed that the sun, moon, and eleven stars bowed down to me."

"Does he think he's better than us?" the brothers complained, getting more and more jealous every day.

The brothers decided they needed to get rid of Joseph once and for all. One day, they set a trap for Joseph, stole his beautiful coat, and threw him into a deep pit. Then, when a group of traders traveled by, the brothers sold Joseph to them. The traders took Joseph far away to the land of Egypt.

That night, Jacob looked around and realized that Joseph was missing. "Where is Joseph?" he asked his children.

The brothers lied to their father, saying that Joseph was lost in the wilderness and gone for good! The brothers held up the coat, which was torn and dirty. "This is all that's left of him!" they said, pretending to cry.

Imagine Imagine yourself feeling jealous when Joseph shared his dreams while wearing his fancy coat.

▶ What do you think Joseph's dreams meant, and why did they make his brothers so angry?

▶ What do you imagine Joseph was thinking and feeling when he realized that his brothers had set a trap for him?

> Think of a time when you were jealous of someone else. Why did you feel that way?

Make Create a coat of many colors.

▶ Imagine that you are Jacob, designing a colorful coat for Joseph. Choose the colors you want to use, and roll out the play dough to be your make-believe fabric.

▶ Use the play dough "fabric" to mold the coat on the doll or action figure.

▶ Give Joseph a twirl to show off his new colorful coat.

You'll Need
- colorful play dough
- a plastic doll or action figure

Play Bring Joseph's dreams to life as a puppet play.

▶ Photocopy or trace and color the dream puppet props from the Joseph's Dream Template (page 45).

▶ Cut out each of the items on the template.

▶ Attach them to chopsticks or straws to make them into puppets.

▶ Find a good table or chair to be a puppet stage. Sit behind the table or chair so that you can create the puppet performance in front of you for your audience.

You'll Need
- Joseph's Dream Template (page 45)
- crayons
- scissors
- tape
- chopsticks or straws
- the Joseph doll with coat (from the MAKE activity above)

> Do your dreams ever tell a story? Do you remember your dreams when you wake up?

▶ Bring the first dream to life. Hold the tall sheaf of wheat in the center. Move the bowing sheaf puppets forward and back to make them bow down to the tall sheaf of wheat.

▶ Bring the second dream to life. Use the sun, moon, and star puppets to bow down to the Joseph doll.

Joseph's Dream Template

Cut out each of the shapes below and attach them to chopsticks or straws using tape. Use them as puppets in the PLAY activity on page 44.

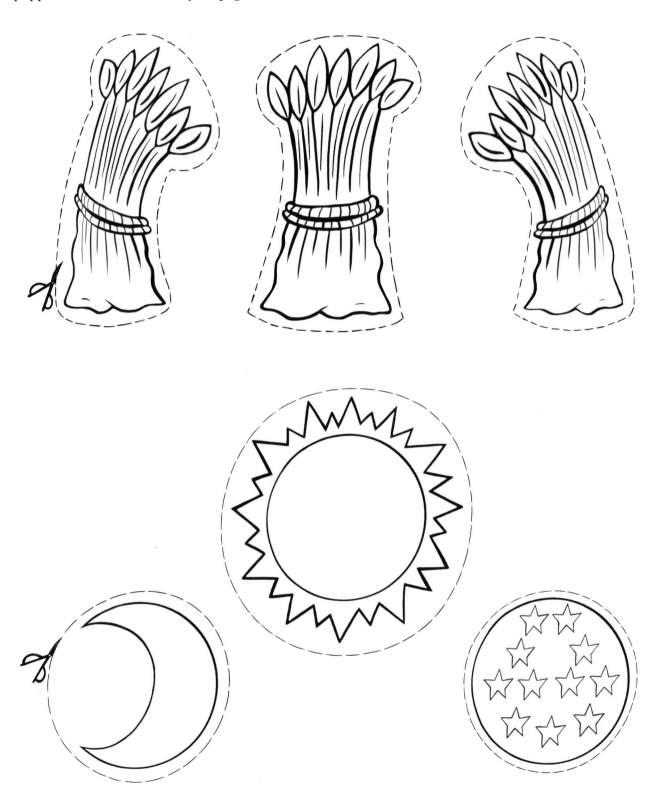

CHAPTER 10

Joseph Has a Plan

Genesis 41:1–44:17 • *Parashat Mikeitz* • מִקֵּץ

**Become a royal advisor to Pharaoh, the king of Egypt,
and save everyone from running out of food.**

How have you helped solve a big problem?

Pharaoh, the king of Egypt, had a mysterious dream one night. "I dreamed that seven skinny cows ate seven fat cows. What could it mean?" he cried. "Find someone who can figure this out!"

Pharaoh's advisors heard about a newcomer who could explain the meaning of dreams . . . it was Joseph! "Tell me what my dream means!" Pharaoh begged.

Joseph understood right away: Egypt would have seven years with lots of food (like the seven fat cows), followed by seven years when food would become hard to find (like the seven skinny cows).

"Joseph, I need you. Become a member of my royal team, and make a plan to save us!" Pharaoh announced.

During the seven good years, Joseph helped store lots of food, so that Egypt had enough when crops became hard to find.

Back home in Canaan, Joseph's family struggled to eat when the food ran out. "What are we going to do? We're so hungry!" Joseph's brothers groaned.

"I hear that there's still food in Egypt," Jacob told them. "Go there and find us something to eat."

When the brothers arrived in Egypt, Joseph recognized them right away. Joseph was still mad at them, but he decided to keep his feelings hidden. "You'll be my guests for dinner!" Joseph proclaimed.

His brothers didn't recognize him, believing that he was an Egyptian prince. Joseph tested his brothers to see if they had changed. He hid a beautiful cup in the bag of his youngest brother, Benjamin. As the brothers were leaving the palace, Joseph yelled, "Wait! My special cup is missing! Guards, check their bags!"

When the cup was found in Benjamin's bag, Joseph told his guards to take Benjamin away to jail. Would the brothers let him go, or would they speak up to protect him?

Imagine **Imagine yourself helping to save Egypt after explaining Pharaoh's dream.**

▶ How do you think you would feel being all alone in Egypt, away from your family, after your brothers were so mean to you?

▶ How would it have felt to speak to Pharaoh for the first time? What do you think it would be like to go from being a stranger from another land to being part of Pharaoh's royal team?

▶ How do you think you would have felt at the moment of seeing your brothers again in Egypt?

 Explore **Exercise your rationing skills as you imagine how Joseph came up with his plan to save Egypt.**

▶ Fill seven bowls each with four pieces of the food item, and leave seven bowls empty.

▶ Imagine that the seven full bowls represent the seven years of food in Egypt, and the seven empty bowls represent the seven years of famine.

▶ Imagine yourself as Joseph. How can you save Egypt and make sure there is enough food for all fourteen years?

> ▶ Experiment with dividing the total amount of food you have evenly across fourteen bowls instead of seven.
>
> > ▶ Once you've divided up the food, eat some of it as a snack. You can enjoy a big snack now or save some for later in the week!

You'll Need
• 14 bowls or containers
• 28 small pieces of one food type (for example, jelly beans, cereal pieces, or grapes)

> Think of a time you saved something for later instead of enjoying it right away. Why did you make that choice?

Make Create a costume for Joseph, and set the scene of his royal ceremony.

▶ Cut two long rectangular strips from the construction paper. Attach the two strips together, so that the long shape can fit around your head.

▶ Decorate it using markers or crayons.

▶ Staple the paper to fit your head, and wear it as a crown.

▶ Make a royal ring by wrapping a pipe cleaner around your finger.

▶ Decide on a chair to use as a throne. Decorate it using a blanket and pillows.

You'll Need
- construction paper
- crayons or markers
- stapler
- pipe cleaner
- a chair
- blanket
- pillows

Play Act out the moment when Joseph becomes a member of Pharaoh's royal team.

▶ Decide who will play Pharaoh and who will play Joseph. (Use the costume and throne you created for Joseph in the MAKE activity above.)

▶ Pharaoh can announce Joseph: "Presenting Joseph, explainer of dreams!"

▶ Joseph walks in and sits on the throne.

▶ Pharaoh puts the crown on Joseph's head. He puts the ring on Joseph's finger.

▶ What do you think Pharaoh says during the ceremony? Add your own dialogue here. (For example, "I'm so happy to welcome you to my team, Joseph!")

▶ Joseph can say, "I will help you save Egypt!"

▶ Now switch roles and act out the scene again.

> Have you ever helped someone else solve a problem? What did you do? How did it feel to help?

For Groups:

With multiple players, you can have half of the group play Joseph and half of the group play Pharaoh. You can also start with two people acting out the scene while the rest of the group watches as the audience. Take turns playing each of the roles.

CHAPTER 11

The Case of the Stolen Cup

Genesis 44:18–47:27 • *Parashat Vayigash* • וַיִּגַּשׁ

Host a big dinner, hide your beautiful cup in Benjamin's
bag, and reunite with your long-lost brothers.

Would you help someone in need, even if they did something horrible to you?

Judah couldn't believe he was eating dinner at the Egyptian palace. Back home, there was no food to eat, so he and his brothers were so excited to be invited for a royal meal soon after they arrived looking for food.

After filling their bellies, the brothers were getting ready to leave when they heard a booming voice. "Wait! My special cup is missing! Guards, check their bags!" said the Egyptian prince.

The brothers stood frozen. Judah was shocked when the guards pulled the cup out of the bag of his youngest brother, Benjamin. What would happen to Benjamin? Would Judah leave his brother behind, just like they left Joseph so many years before?

Judah bravely stepped forward. "Don't take Benjamin. Take me instead!"

The Egyptian prince started to cry. "Brothers, don't you see? It's me, Joseph!"

Judah was in shock. His long-lost brother was standing right in front of him. Judah felt ashamed for what he and his brothers had done to Joseph. "I see you've changed since you tricked me," Joseph said. "Don't worry. After all, if I hadn't been sent to Egypt, I never would have been able to save all of us!"

Joseph hugged his brothers. "Go tell father that I'm here!" Joseph said. "Bring him to Egypt. The whole family can live close together again. I will take care of all of you."

The brothers returned home to share their discovery. "Father, we found Joseph! He helped Pharaoh save everyone!" Judah said.

Jacob couldn't believe it. "I have to see him right away!" Judah helped Jacob pack up all of his things, and the family moved to Egypt.

"Joseph . . . is that really you?" Jacob said with tears in his eyes. Jacob held Joseph in a hug for a long time then shouted for everyone to hear, "My children are all together again!"

Imagine Imagine yourself recognizing Joseph after he was gone for a long time.

▶ Why do you think Joseph decided to create his plan and test his brothers?

▶ If you were in Joseph's place, would you forgive your brothers? Why or why not?

 Make Create the cup that Joseph uses to trick his brothers.

▶ Wrap aluminum foil around each of the paper cups.

▶ Turn one cup over, and tape the bottoms of the two cups together. One cup becomes the top of the goblet, while the other becomes the base.

▶ You can use a permanent marker or crayon to add decoration to the outside of the cup.

> **You'll Need**
> • 2 paper cups
> • aluminum foil
> • tape
> • permanent marker

 Play Act out the moment when Joseph tricks his brothers and then reveals his identity.

▶ Set up the table for Joseph's big dinner for his brothers. Put a chair at the head of the table for Joseph to sit on.

▶ Cast a stuffed animal as Benjamin. Seat Benjamin at the table, and put a bag near him.

▶ Decide who will play Joseph and who will play Judah.

▶ Joseph can sneak around the table and hide the cup you made in Benjamin's bag.

> **You'll Need**
> • a table
> • plates
> • a chair
> • stuffed animal
> • backpack or bag
> • the cup (from the MAKE activity above)

Has a friend or family member ever made you feel surprised? What did they do?

▶ Then Joseph can stand up and say, "Benjamin has my cup! Take him away!" What do you think Joseph is feeling at this moment? Show it with your facial expressions and your movements.

▶ Judah can kneel down and say, "Please, Joseph, don't take Benjamin. Take me!" What do you think Judah is feeling at this moment? Show it with your facial expressions and your movements.

▶ Joseph can say, "Brother, it's me, Joseph!"

▶ They hug in reunion!

▶ Now switch roles and act out the scene again.

For Groups:

With multiple players, you can have half of the group play Joseph and half of the group play Judah. Alternatively, you can add characters to the scene by casting additional players in the roles of Benjamin and the other brothers.

Think of a time you were very upset with someone. What did you do? What did you say to them?

CHAPTER 12

Jacob Blesses His Family

Genesis 47:28–50:26 • *Parashat Vaychi* • וַיְחִי

Create your own blessing, and share it aloud like the ones Jacob offers to his family.

What do you say when you find something you thought was lost forever?

Jacob and his family happily lived in Egypt together for many years. Jacob grew very old, surrounded by all of his children and grandchildren. He decided it was time to give them all a gift. Jacob called his children together so that he could bless each of them.

"Gather round, my family. I will give each of you your own unique blessing," he said.

Each of Jacob's children stepped forward when it was their turn. Jacob's voice was quiet and slow, so they each leaned forward as they received their blessing, sitting close to their father to hear the unique words he chose just for them. Jacob used the qualities of different animals to bless them, comparing Judah to a lion, Naphtali to a gazelle, and Benjamin to a wolf.

"I want to bless my grandchildren, too," Jacob said. "Bring your children to me, Joseph."

Joseph had married an Egyptian woman named Asenath, and together they had two sons. Joseph brought his children, Ephraim and Manasseh, to visit Jacob and receive their own blessing. Jacob put his hands across the heads of Ephraim and Manasseh as he blessed them. "Your families will grow and grow to fill the world," he said as he looked at them with a loving smile.

After he was done giving out blessings, Jacob remembered the blessing that God made to his grandparents, Abraham and Sarah, so many years before—the promise that generations of their family would grow into a great big community and fill the world with love, stories, and tradition. He looked around and saw that it was beginning to come true. "One day, we'll all find our way back home to the land of Canaan," Jacob thought.

But for now, Jacob felt grateful for his own blessing: a large and wonderful family, happily living all together again.

Imagine Imagine yourself getting your own unique blessing from Jacob.

▶ How do you think Jacob felt seeing Joseph again after so many years?

▶ Why do you think it was important to Jacob to give each of his children and grandchildren a unique blessing? How do you think he decided what to say to each of them?

> If you were an animal, which animal would you be, and why? What qualities do you have that make you like that animal?

Make Create your own blessing inspired by Jacob's blessings of his sons.

▶ Photocopy or trace the Blessing Template (page 54).

▶ Think of an animal that has traits or qualities you would like to have. Use this animal to inspire a blessing that you write.

▶ Think of two traits of that animal that you admire. Think of what a person can do with those traits.

> **You'll Need**
> • Blessing Template (page 54)
> • crayons or markers

▶ Fill in the blanks of the template with your answers to write your own blessing. Here's an example: "May you be like an eagle: swift and brave so that you can fly high above the clouds!" For children too young to write, ask them the prompt out loud, and write their answers in the template.

> When have you heard someone reciting a blessing? Why do you think people offer blessings?

▶ Practice saying the full blessing aloud together.

▶ Draw a picture of your animal on the template.

Play Act out the moment of Jacob giving a blessing to his grandsons, Ephraim and Manasseh.

▶ Find two stuffed animals to be Ephraim and Manasseh.

▶ Sit in front of them, and put your hands on the heads of the stuffed animals.

> **You'll Need**
> • two stuffed animals
> • your blessing (from the MAKE activity above)

▶ Recite the animal blessing you created in the previous activity, and give the blessing to the two stuffed animals, imagining they are Ephraim and Manasseh. You can also create two different blessings, one for each of the stuffed animals.

Blessing Template

Create a blessing and decorate it, following the instructions in the MAKE activity.

May you be like a _____ :
[animal]

_____ and _____
[adjective]   [adjective]

So that you _____
[action phrase]

Completing Genesis
A Celebration Ritual

After completing each book of the Torah, we celebrate what we have explored together, and we build excitement for the adventures we'll take in the next book. You've just finished the Book of Genesis! Mark this milestone together using the ritual below.

Unroll the Scroll

Imagine that you are the big scroll of the Torah, the rolled-up piece of parchment paper that holds all of these stories. Stand really tall, with your arms at your sides. On the count of three, do *one* giant spin to pretend that you are unrolling the scroll to the next book of the Torah. One, two, three, spin!

Shout a Cheer

Traditionally, we say, "*Chazak, chazak, v'nit'chazeik!*" when we finish a book of the Torah. In Hebrew, this means "Be strong, be strong, and we'll be strong together!" You can say these words together or come up with your own cheer (for example, "I did it! We did it! We'll all keep exploring together!").

Celebrate

Have a party to celebrate everything you've learned and explored. You could have a special meal, decorate the room, make a playlist of songs inspired by your Genesis adventures, or jump around for a celebratory dance party. Plan how you want to mark the moment together, and celebrate your own way!

EXODUS
OUT OF EGYPT
AND AWAY WE GO

Travel across the sand to Egypt, where Jacob's family grew and grew to become the Israelite people, forced to work for Pharaoh as slaves. Join them as Moses leads them to freedom and into the desert. Travel with them to the base of Mount Sinai, and follow as they make their way across the wilderness into the unknown. Watch as they build a traveling temple and learn what it means to become a community.

You'll sing and dance as you cross the Sea of Reeds, build your own miniature Mount Sinai, and create your own uniform to imagine working inside the temple in the desert.

CHAPTER 13

The Baby in the Basket

Exodus 1:1–6:1 • *Parashat Sh'mot* • שְׁמוֹת

Build an Egyptian city, guide baby Moses down the Nile River, and experience the wonder of the Burning Bush.

What would you do if you saw someone being treated unfairly?

Jacob's family grew in Egypt to become a large people called the Israelites. Everything was fine until a new Pharaoh became the leader. "The Israelites must work for me," he declared. "They are my slaves now, and they will build my cities, brick by brick."

Soon Pharaoh became worried that there were way too many Israelites, and one day they would become too powerful for him to control. So he made a plan. "Starting today, there can be no more new Israelite baby boys in all of Egypt!" he said.

An Israelite named Yoheved made a plan to keep her baby safe from Pharaoh. "I will put you in a basket and send you down the Nile River," she whispered. "I believe you'll find a better place, where you can be free."

The baby's sister, Miriam, bravely helped guide the floating basket. "This is your destiny," Miriam told the baby.

Pharaoh's daughter, Batya, was taking a swim when she noticed something strange. "There's a baby in this basket!" she gasped. "Don't worry, I will keep you safe. I will name you Moses."

As Moses grew up in the palace, he knew in his heart that he was an Israelite. "I can't live here while the Israelites are forced to work in the hot sun!" Moses said.

He ran far away from Egypt, all the way to the hills of Midian. There, he became a part of the local community, and he married a shepherdess named Zipporah.

One day, while taking care of the sheep, Moses noticed something incredible: a bush was bright with fire, but the flame wasn't destroying the branches. Suddenly, he heard a voice from within the bush. "Moses—you must return to Egypt and tell Pharaoh to let my people go. I will be with you every step of the way," the voice said.

Moses was nervous, but he knew it was time to go back. He turned around and began the long journey back to Egypt to free his people.

Imagine Imagine yourself as Miriam and as Moses in this story.

▶ How do you think Miriam felt when she saw Pharaoh's daughter bring her baby brother into the palace?

▶ How do you think Moses felt when the voice in the bush told him he needed to go back to Egypt and stand up to Pharaoh?

> Have you ever taken care of something or someone you love? What did you do? How did it make you feel?

Make Build a city in ancient Egypt to explore where the Israelites lived.

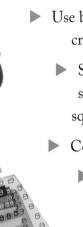

▶ Use blocks or plastic building bricks to create a pyramid structure.

   ▶ Start with a large square. Stack a smaller square on top of the large square.

▶ Continue to add smaller square layers to stack the pyramid high.

   ▶ Use blocks to create lots of buildings of different shapes and sizes in ancient Egypt. Add a Nile River using a towel.

You'll Need
- blocks or plastic building bricks
- a towel

Play Act out the journey that Baby Moses takes down the Nile River.

▶ Create a long river using several bedsheets, blankets, and pillows.

▶ Cast a stuffed animal as Baby Moses, and place him in a basket or container. Add a small blanket around him.

▶ Person 1 takes on the role of Miriam. Miriam can whisper a message of love into the basket. What words of love might Miriam whisper into the basket?

▶ Person 1 pretends to float the basket down the entire path of the Nile River you created.

You'll Need
- bedsheets
- blankets
- pillows
- stuffed animal
- basket or container

▶ Person 2 takes on the role of Pharaoh's daughter. Find the basket and act surprised when you see the baby inside. Take him out and say, "I will call you Moses, and I will take care of you!" What might Pharaoh's daughter say to make the baby feel safe?

▶ Now switch roles and act out the scene again!

> Have you ever felt scared to do something? How did you find the courage to do it anyway?

For Groups:

With multiple players, everyone can take a turn guiding Baby Moses down the river, or you can pass the basket from person to person. You can also start with two people acting out the scene while the rest of the group watches as the audience. Take turns playing each of the roles.

Make Create a burning bush that can light up the room.

▶ Draw the shape of a bush with leaves and branches on it. Now, draw fire around the bush. Color it in with yellow and orange markers.

▶ Roll the paper up with the color on the outside, and tape it to create a cylindrical shape.

> **You'll Need**
> - paper
> - markers
> - tape
> - flashlight or phone flashlight

▶ Go into a dark space. Put the flashlight underneath the paper tube, and light up your burning bush!

▶ Sit around the burning bush together.

▶ Imagine a voice coming from inside the bush! Take turns delivering the message: "Moses, go back to Egypt and tell Pharaoh to let my people go!"

CHAPTER 14

Let My People Go!

Exodus 6:2–9:35 • *Parashat Va'eira* • וָאֵרָא

**Return to Egypt, help make wild things happen,
and try to change Pharaoh's mind.**

What would you do if you had to change someone's mind?

Moses walked across the desert sand back to Egypt, thinking about what he would say to Pharaoh. Along the way, his brother, Aaron, came to meet him. "I knew you'd come back, Moses!" Aaron said as he hugged his long-lost brother.

When it was time to go speak to Pharaoh, Moses felt nervous. "I'm not good at giving speeches. I get tongue-tied," he said.

"Don't worry; I'll help you speak up to Pharaoh," Aaron said.

Together they climbed the tall stairway to the palace and walked straight into Pharaoh's throne room. "Let my people go!" Moses said to Pharaoh. "They deserve to be free. You can't force them to work for you anymore!"

"No, Moses, they belong to me," Pharaoh said sternly.

Moses tried asking many times, but it was no use. Pharaoh just kept saying no. Moses started feeling discouraged, but then he remembered the voice from the burning bush—God's voice—saying, "I will be with you every step of the way."

With some help from God, wild things started to happen in Egypt—plagues meant to convince Pharaoh to let the Israelites go. Aaron dipped his staff into the Nile River, and the waters suddenly turned completely blood red. Then, millions of frogs appeared everywhere across the land, hopping on tables, in beds, and even in the palace! Lice swarmed, wild animals roamed the streets, and hail fell from the sky. Even after all that, Pharaoh still didn't change his mind.

Imagine Imagine yourself trying to convince Pharaoh to let the people go.

▶ How do you think Moses felt returning to the palace where he grew up as a prince to convince Pharaoh to free the Israelites?

▶ How would you try to convince Pharaoh? What would you say?

> Have you ever tried to convince someone to change their mind? How did you do it?

Make Use your staff to make the river turn red.

▶ Take a piece of paper towel, and fold it in half.

▶ On the outside, use the permanent marker to draw the shape of the staff.

▶ On the inside, use the red marker to color in the whole inside of the paper towel.

▶ When you are ready, drop the folded paper (with the staff side up) into the water, and watch as the water quickly turns red.

You'll Need
• paper towel
• permanent marker
• washable red marker
• a bowl filled with water

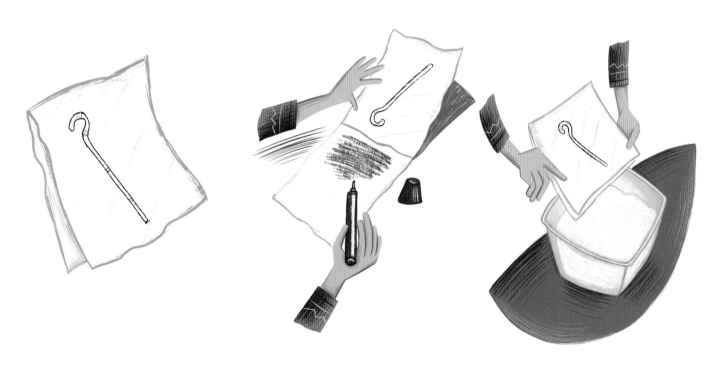

Play Act out the moment when Moses tries to convince Pharaoh to let the people go!

▶ Decide who will play Moses and who will play Pharaoh.

▶ Pharaoh sits down on a throne in one part of the room.

▶ Moses walks toward Pharaoh.

▶ Moses tries as many ways as you can think of to convince Pharaoh to let the people be free.

▶ Pharaoh says, "No, no, no!"

▶ Now switch roles so that everyone has a turn to play both parts!

For Groups:

With multiple players, you can have half of the group play Moses and half of the group play Pharaoh. You can also start with two people acting out the scene while the rest of the group watches as the audience. Take turns playing each of the roles.

> Have you ever been stubborn about changing your mind? What did the other person do to try to make you change?

CHAPTER 15

Moses, Lead the Way!

Exodus 10:1–13:16 • *Parashat Bo* • בֹּא

Explore the darkness, pack up your stuff, and get ready to leave Egypt!

Have you ever packed up very quickly for a trip?

"Pharaoh, will you let the Israelites go?" Moses asked again. Pharaoh crossed his arms and shook his head.

"Forget it, Moses!" he shouted stubbornly.

Moses sighed and said, "Then God will continue to make wild things happen to your people."

All of a sudden, swarms of locusts buzzed overhead across all of Egypt. It was so loud that the Egyptians couldn't hear each other over the sounds of the flying insects.

Then, a total darkness covered the land of Egypt, day and night. The Egyptians couldn't see their hands in front of their faces, and they kept bumping into each other. All of Egypt shut down. When Pharaoh still refused to change his mind, even more terrible things happened. Finally, it was too much for Pharaoh and the rest of the Egyptians to take. "Enough! Take your people and go," Pharaoh told Moses.

This was it! The moment of freedom had arrived. The Israelites were in disbelief. Were they really free to leave? Moses told the Israelites to pack up very quickly and get ready to go. "It's time. Take that dough out of the oven—we don't have time to make bread!" he shouted.

The Israelites had invented the world's first matzah. They took it with them for the journey ahead. All together, the Israelites followed Moses out of Egypt, finally on their way to freedom.

Imagine Imagine yourself quickly packing up to finally leave Egypt.

▶ How do you think the Israelites felt when they heard that they could finally leave Egypt and be free?

▶ Why do you think they decided to leave Egypt quickly rather than taking their time to prepare?

▶ What do you think the Israelites were feeling when they took their first steps into the wilderness outside of Egypt?

> Think about what it was like when all of Egypt was in total darkness. Do you like being in the dark? What do you do to feel brave in the dark?

Make Create the special staff that Moses used to make incredible things happen in Egypt with God's help.

▶ Use your imagination to decorate the three pieces of paper with one of the wild things that God makes happen in Egypt when Moses and Aaron put the staff in the air. If you need inspiration, here are some ideas:

You'll Need
• 3 sheets of construction paper
• crayons
• tape

- Cover the first piece of paper with drawings of frogs everywhere, or fill the page with green polka dots.

- Cover the second piece of paper with drawings of lice, or fill the page with little black spots.

- Cover the third piece of paper with drawings of fiery hail raining from the sky, or fill the page with orange and blue squiggles.

▶ Roll the construction paper sheets into long, thin tubes, with your drawings facing outward.

▶ Tape the tubes so they stay in place.

▶ Attach the tubes together using tape to make one long staff.

▶ Hold the staff in the air, and imagine using it to bring a total darkness to Egypt for three days. On the count of three, one person can hold up the staff while the other person turns off the lights!

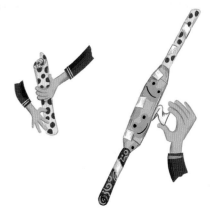

Play Imagine that you are navigating Egypt in total darkness.

▶ One person can be the explorer, and one person can be the guide.

▶ The explorer covers their face with the bandana or cloth. Make sure it totally covers the eyes so that the explorer can't see anything.

> **You'll Need**
> • bandana or cloth

▶ The explorer spins around three times.

▶ The explorer starts navigating the room, with arms stretched out in front and walking slowly.

▶ The other person can help guide and protect the explorer from getting hurt or bumping into anything.

▶ Now switch roles!

> *Have you ever been on a big trip? How did you decide what to pack?*

 Play Pack up your things and imagine leaving Egypt with the Israelites.

▶ The Israelites packed up really quickly and left Egypt in a hurry. If you were leaving your home quickly, what would you take with you?

> **You'll Need**
> • backpack

▶ Set three minutes on the clock. Choose the five most important items that you would decide to pack with you if you were leaving really fast.

▶ Put the items in a backpack.

▶ Once you have packed, everyone can compare items. Share why you chose those five items to bring with you.

> *Have you ever needed to leave somewhere in a hurry? What does it feel like to be in a rush?*

CHAPTER 16

The Israelites and the Sea of Reeds

Exodus 13:17–17:16 • *Parashat B'shalach* • בְּשַׁלַּח

**Try parting the waters of the Sea of Reeds, create a
miniature miracle, and dance your way to freedom!**

Have you ever faced a problem that you didn't know how to solve?

"We're free!" Miriam said as the Israelites journeyed out of Egypt and into the wilderness. She spent the whole day walking across the sand with a big smile across her face.

As the sun went down, Miriam and the rest of the Israelites stopped abruptly in their tracks. They saw the roaring waves of the Sea of Reeds rising in front of them, with no way to get across. Water stretched out as far as their eyes could see. "What are we going to do now?!" Moses said to Miriam, unsure of what to do next.

"We should have stayed in Egypt!" Miriam heard the Israelites shouting at Moses.

"Don't be afraid! God will help us find an answer," Miriam said to her brother.

Moses raised his hands over the water, and it suddenly parted into two walls, with a dry path in the middle for them to cross! As they walked down the path, they could see whales gliding, dolphins jumping, and other sea creatures through the walls of the water. "Grab your tambourines, and let's celebrate with a song!" Miriam said as they reached the other side.

The Israelites felt hungry after walking through the wilderness all day. "What are we going to eat out here in the desert? We should have stayed in Egypt!" they grumbled again as they went to bed hungry.

In the morning, Miriam peeked out of her tent, and her eyes went wide. Covering the entire wilderness was a layer of food that had fallen from the sky. "What is this?" the people asked as they took their first bite.

"This is a food called manna, which God has given us to eat," Moses told them.

As Miriam filled her belly, she knew that the Israelites would be able to find their way through any problem, big or small, along the journey ahead.

Imagine yourself standing at the edge of the Sea of Reeds, unsure of how you would get across.

▶ How do you think the Israelites felt when they arrived at the Sea of Reeds with no way across? How would you feel?

▶ What do you think it felt like to cross through the Sea of Reeds and see the water turn into two walls? What do you think the people saw when they looked at the water walls?

▶ What song would *you* sing as you were crossing the sea?

> Have you ever been near the ocean or a large lake? How did it feel to look out at all that water?

 Experiment with parting the waters and crossing through.

▶ Think about how water behaves. Use your hands to see if you can create a dry path in the middle of a bowl of water. Is it possible to make it move a certain way or split apart?

You'll Need
• bowl filled with water
• utensils (spatula, spoon, etc.)
• ice cubes

▶ Try using different utensils to make the water separate. What does the water do?

> Have you ever been scared to travel from one place to another? How did you find the courage to go?

▶ Now, gather a bunch of ice cubes in a pile. Use your hands or the utensils to make two rows, with a path down the center. Was it easier to separate the water or the ice cubes? Why? How do you imagine the Sea of Reeds parting into walls with a dry path to follow in between?

Play Imagine leading the Israelites through the Sea of Reeds, and make some music as you celebrate.

▶ Put two chairs about six feet apart, facing another two chairs six feet apart.

▶ Hang a bedsheet across each set of chairs, creating a tunnel between them. Imagine that this tunnel is the path that the Israelites walked through the Sea of Reeds and the bedsheets are the two walls of water.

> **You'll Need**
> - 4 chairs
> - 2 bedsheets
> - an instrument or an object that makes noise (for example, pot lids)

> Why do you think people often use music to celebrate? What music do you like to listen to when you dance?

▶ Take an instrument, and have a dance party as you cross through the tunnel!

CHAPTER 17

A Big Day at Sinai

Exodus 18:1–20:23 • *Parashat Yitro* • יִתְרוֹ

Create your own Mount Sinai, bring it to life, and explore the Ten Commandments.

Have you ever seen something that made you feel amazed?

After traveling in the wilderness for seven weeks, the Israelites stopped to set up camp at the base of Mount Sinai. "This is the spot," Moses told them. "Set up your tents, and rest your feet. We'll be staying here for a while."

Moses looked out in the distance and saw a few people approaching their campsite. Could it really be his family? He missed them so much. He hadn't seen them since he went back to Egypt. Yes! It was them. "Moses! We're together again!" said his wife, Zipporah, as she hugged him. Zipporah had traveled from her homeland of Midian with their sons to join the Israelites on their journey.

Moses gathered the Israelites together for an important announcement: "Today is a very special day. Here at Mount Sinai, we will get a gift: God's instructions for how we live together on our own as free people."

Suddenly, the sky filled with thunder and lightning, and fire and smoke appeared on the top of the mountain. A very loud blast was sounded, and the whole mountain shook and trembled. It was an incredible sight! "I am your God, who brought you out of Egypt," Moses heard a loud voice say from the top of the mountain.

God announced the Ten Commandments to Moses, the most important rules and ideas the Israelites would need to follow:

1. I am your one and only God.
2. Don't create any sculptures or objects to be your god.
3. Be careful with the words you use.
4. Make time to rest each week.
5. Respect your parents and caregivers.
6. Don't hurt other people.
7. Keep your promises to the people you love.
8. Don't take what isn't yours.
9. Don't tell lies.
10. Don't be jealous of other people.

Moses shared what he heard with the people. As the Israelites listened, they agreed to follow these commandments. They stood together, looking up at the mountain, feeling amazement and wonder.

Imagine Imagine yourself standing at the base of Mount Sinai, watching the sky fill with lightning and smoke.

► How do you think you'd feel watching Mount Sinai light up with fire, smoke, lightning, and thunder?

► Why do you think it was important for the people to receive the Ten Commandments all together, as a community?

> If you could add an eleventh commandment, what would it be?

Make Create your own tabletop Mount Sinai using paper and tape.

► Crumple up a few pieces of yellow or tan construction paper, and then carefully open them up again. Repeat this a few times so that the paper has a rocky texture.

► Wrap the construction paper around the cardboard, and tape it to secure it. This will be the ground on which you build your mountain.

► Now, crumple a sheet of newspaper into a ball. Repeat this a few times to create a bunch of newspaper balls.

You'll Need

- yellow or tan construction paper
- a piece of cardboard, approximately 12 x 12 inches
- newspaper or other scrap paper
- tape
- brown construction paper or brown grocery bags

► Put more newspaper balls on the yellow ground, and tape them down and to each other.

▶ Stack more newspaper balls to create the shape of a mountain, taping each one to the structure to secure it.

▶ Now, crumple up a few pieces of brown construction paper (or cut up brown paper grocery bags). Carefully open them up again. These pieces will be used to "skin" the outside of the mountain. Sculpt them around your mound of newspaper balls, and tape them in place.

▶ Make sure to cover the whole mound with textured brown construction paper.

 Play **Imagine the moment that the Israelites received the Ten Commandments at Mount Sinai.**

▶ Put your small toy figures in front of your mountain, imagining they are the community of Israelites at Mount Sinai. Choose toys to be Moses, Miriam, and Aaron. You can also have toys stand in as Moses's wife and sons.

▶ Create a small fire shape using the orange play dough or crumpled-up orange paper.

▶ First, make the fire appear at the top of the mountain, like the one the Israelites saw in the story.

You'll Need
• the mountain (from the MAKE activity on page 71)
• small toy figures
• orange play dough or orange paper
• cotton balls
• aluminum foil

▶ Now, hold the cloud of smoke (a bunch of cotton balls), making it fly and hover around the mountain. Create the sound effects of the fire and smoke with your voice. What sounds do they make?

▶ Now, take the aluminum foil and shake it to make the sound of thunder that the Israelites felt and heard before they received the Ten Commandments.

▶ Use your voice to create the sound of the loud blast.

▶ Finally, pick up the mountain at the base and make it tremble and shake!

> Do you have rules that are shared by everyone in your family or in your classroom? Why are community rules important to create and follow?

CHAPTER 18

Moses on the Mountain

Exodus 21:1–24:18 • *Parashat Mishpatim* • מִשְׁפָּטִים

Climb to the top of Mount Sinai to receive the Ten Commandments on stone tablets, and stay there for forty days and forty nights.

What is the best present you've ever received?

The people stood looking up at the mountain in wonder. God shared many new rules and laws for the Israelite people to follow as they created their own community together away from Egypt. God also told them where their journey through the wilderness would lead them: to build a new home in the land of Canaan. The Israelite people raised their voices all together and said, "We will do all of these things that God has commanded!"

God told Moses to come up to the top of the mountain. "This is only the beginning. God will give us these commandments written on beautiful stone tablets. I will be back with an even greater gift for you," Moses told the people.

"Aaron, I'm putting you in charge while I'm gone," Moses said to his brother as he began to climb the mountain. The Israelites watched as Moses went higher and higher, until he disappeared behind the thick cloud at the peak.

The people stood at the bottom of the mountain, looking up. "What will Moses do up there? When will he come back?" they wondered.

With each step he took, Moses felt more on his own. He thought about his wife, Zipporah, his two sons, his sister, Miriam, and his brother, Aaron, staring up at him from their tents. Moses went inside the cloud, where he stayed for forty days and forty nights while the people waited for him to return.

Imagine Imagine yourself camping at the base of Mount Sinai, waiting for Moses to come back.

▶ Why do you think Moses needed to go up the mountain and into the cloud on his own?

▶ How do you think Moses's sons felt when their dad left to go up the mountain?

▶ Why do you think the Israelites needed rules to follow now that they were free from Egypt?

> Have you ever climbed or driven to the top of a mountain or a big hill, like Moses does in the story? What did you see from up there?

 Make Create and decorate your own version of the Ten Commandments tablets.

▶ Cut two rectangular pieces of cardboard of equal size.

▶ Write the numbers 1 through 5 vertically on one piece of cardboard.

▶ Write the numbers 6 through 10 vertically on the other piece of cardboard.

▶ Decorate the two tablets using markers and crayons.

▶ Brainstorm a list of the rules, values, and guiding activities that are important in your family or classroom. They can include things that you love to do together, rules that you follow, and values that matter to you. You can write them as commands; for example: "We read stories together every night," or "We always share with our friends."

> **You'll Need**
> • 2 pieces of cardboard
> • markers and crayons

> Imagine a house or classroom without any rules. What would be great about it? What would be hard about it?

▶ On your cardboard tablets, write out your list of ten ideas, five on each one. You can also draw pictures to represent each idea instead of writing them.

> **TIP:** Save your Ten Commandments tablets to use again in chapters 19, 21, and 22

Play Create the cloud on Mount Sinai, and act out the moment of climbing the mountain and receiving the tablets.

▶ Create a pile of pillows and blankets. Construct the pillows like a mini-mountain.

▶ Hide the commandments tablets underneath the pillows.

▶ Say goodbye to someone at the bottom of the mountain, and climb up to the top.

▶ When you get to the top, wrap a bedsheet over you to imagine you are entering the cloud.

▶ Use flashlights to make the cloud feel more magical.

▶ Find the tablets and hold them up in the air.

You'll Need
• pillows
• blankets
• the commandments tablets (from the MAKE activity on page 74)
• bedsheet
• flashlights
• cardboard tube or rolled-up piece of paper

> How does it feel to do something all by yourself?

▶ Use the cardboard tube or rolled-up paper as a shofar (ram's horn instrument) or trumpet, making a loud sound by blowing into it.

▶ Now, share your ideas from the commandments you brainstormed, using your tube as a microphone.

CHAPTER 19

Building in the Wilderness

Exodus 25:1–27:19 • *Parashat T'rumah* • תְּרוּמָה

Build your own Menorah, construct a special Ark, and think about how we create community spaces to share gratitude together.

Where do you keep your most important and precious objects?

While sitting inside the cloud on the top of Mount Sinai for forty days and forty nights, Moses received the Torah from God—a special set of stories, ideas, and instructions that would become the most important guide for the Israelite people.

Each day, Moses would listen and learn from God, trying to remember the details of all of the instructions in his head. "Here's what you need to do when you get back to the people," God said, sharing these instructions.

First, the Israelites needed to work as a team to build a safe place to keep the Ten Commandments while they traveled in the wilderness. They also needed to create a very special place to show gratitude and celebrate holidays. Everyone would need to do their part to make the project happen. "But we're on the move. How can we build a special gathering place if we are going to be walking through the wilderness?" Moses wondered.

God told him that the Israelites needed to build the Tabernacle (called the *Mishkan* in Hebrew), a portable temple that would travel with them wherever they went. The Israelites each needed to bring supplies as gifts that would be used to build the Tabernacle. It would be a place to say prayers, sing songs, and offer thanks. "What else will go inside this special place?" Moses asked.

Inside the Tabernacle, they would put the Ark, a golden box with two winged-angel statues on top. This box would be the safe place for the Ten Commandments. The people would also build a Menorah to light each day to burn bright and shine through the night.

Imagine Imagine yourself getting instructions to build the Tabernacle in the wilderness.

▶ How do you think Moses felt trying to remember all of the instructions that God gave him to bring back to the Israelites?

▶ Why do you think it was important for everyone to give some supplies as gifts to make the Tabernacle? What do you think you would bring to help build it?

> Where do you keep very special objects? How do you keep them safe?

 Make Get creative using blocks and toys to build your own Ark.

▶ Take a look at the shape of the Ark in the illustration. Look for the main box, the poles to carry it, and the two angel sculptures on top.

▶ Think about what building materials you can collect to create this shape. What can you use to create a box that actually opens and closes?

▶ Experiment using different materials to see what works best to create a structure that can hold something inside and can be carried around like the Ark.

▶ Next construct poles around or underneath the box so that you can carry it.

> **You'll Need**
> • various toys and supplies for building (like blocks, plastic building bricks, cardboard, tape, aluminum foil)
> • paper or your cardboard Ten Commandments (from the MAKE activity in chapter 18)

> **Tip:** Save your Ten Commandments tablets to use again in chapters 21 and 22.

> Have you ever seen an Ark where a Torah is kept? What does it look like?

▶ Find two toys that can be the two angels on the top of your Ark.

▶ Use two small pieces of paper to be your Ten Commandments, and put them safely inside your Ark. Alternatively, you can use the commandments you created in chapter 18.

▶ Now, see if you can safely carry and transport the Ark you built. Lift your Ark using the poles you made. Together with another person, carefully and slowly carry your Ark around the room.

▶ Experiment with the best way to hold and carry your Ark to keep it safe. Work together as a team to make sure you can carry it smoothly and safely.

Play Use your bodies to create the special objects for the Tabernacle.

▶ Look at the pictures of the Menorah and the Ark.

▶ Using your body, create the shape of the Menorah. Stand really tall, make your arms into a cactus shape, and hold three fingers up on each hand (the Menorah in the Tabernacle had three branches on either side, unlike a *hanukkiyah*, which has four on each side).

> When do you light candles? Why do you think we light candles on special occasions like holidays and birthdays? How do they make you feel when they are lit?

▶ Now, see if you can make the shape of the sculpture on top of the Ark using your bodies. Face each other, and use your arms to create the shape of the angel wings, with the tips of your fingers touching. Try to hold really still like a sculpture!

• There are different opinions about the shape of this sculpture. Some people think the angels faced each other, and others think the angels looked down at the Ark. Use your bodies to try out these different shapes.

CHAPTER 20

The Tabernacle Team

Exodus 27:20–30:10 • *Parashat T'tzaveh* • תְּצַוֶּה

Design a special outfit including a breastplate and a headdress, get dressed
up, create a ritual, and imagine becoming one of the Israelite priests.

Have you ever been part of a team wearing a uniform?

While sitting inside the cloud on the top of Mount Sinai, Moses got instructions from God on what
to do when he returned to his people. Once they built the Tabernacle, the portable temple in the
wilderness, the Israelites would need a team of people to lead the rituals and activities inside.

"Who should be on this team, and what should they do?" Moses asked.

"Your brother, Aaron, and his children will take on this job," God said.

Their temple team would be called the *kohanim*, or "priests." They would make sure that the
Menorah always remained lit and shining brightly. They would need to wear a uniform while they
worked inside the Tabernacle. Aaron's uniform featured a large metal plate tied around his chest,
decorated with twelve precious stones, one for each tribe; a fancy robe; and a tall hat.

"Will we just give them these jobs, and they'll start right away?" Moses asked.

God gave Moses detailed instructions for a grand ceremony to prepare Aaron and his sons for this
important responsibility. They would put on their uniforms for the first time and then stay inside the
Tabernacle for seven whole days.

Moses asked a lot of questions and tried hard to memorize every detail so he could tell everyone
back at the camp everything he learned. There were so many details to learn and remember! He
couldn't wait until the day when the Tabernacle was finally built and the Israelite people were on their
way through the wilderness. But for now, he kept his head in the clouds.

Imagine **Imagine yourself as one of the *kohanim*, putting on the special uniform.**

▶ Why do you think the *kohanim* had to wear a fancy uniform when they went inside the Tabernacle?

▶ How do you think the *kohanim* felt when they put on this uniform?

> Why are special clothes for certain jobs important?

 Make **Use craft supplies to create Aaron's breastplate.**

▶ Draw three vertical rows of four squares on a piece of white paper.

▶ Imagine that each square holds a precious stone. Choose a different color for each stone, and color in the square.

▶ Cut out your twelve "stone" squares.

▶ Now, take a yellow sheet of construction paper, and use tape to attach it to a piece of cardboard (cut to be the same size as the paper).

▶ Tape your "stones" onto the yellow piece of paper in three vertical rows of four squares.

▶ Punch two holes in the cardboard on either side at the top. Attach string through the holes of the cardboard, or use masking tape, so that the breastplate can be worn across the chest like a necklace.

You'll Need
● a sheet of white paper
● crayons
● scissors
● a sheet of yellow construction paper
● a piece of cardboard
● hole puncher
● masking tape or string

> What jobs can you think of that require a uniform? Do kids ever wear uniforms?

Make   Use craft supplies to create the Aaron's headdress.

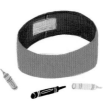

▶ Cut a piece of construction paper in half the long way (vertically).

▶ Fit it to your head as a crown, and staple the two pieces together.

▶ Cut the two other sheets of construction paper into long thin strips.

▶ Using the stapler, attach one strip from one side of the crown to the other, in a rainbow arc shape.

▶ Attach another strip as a rainbow arc across the opposite side, so that the two strips meet in the middle like an X.

▶ Attach a few more strips in this way, starting from an empty space on the side of the crown and attaching across in a rainbow arc. This will create the shape of a turban headpiece.

You'll Need
- 3 sheets of construction paper (various colors)
- scissors
- a stapler

Tip:
Save your *kohein* uniform to use it again for the activities in chapter 25.

Play   Pretend to be Aaron by putting on your special uniform.

▶ Wrap the towel around your waist like a skirt.

▶ Attach the breastplate to your chest. You can use masking tape or string to attach it around your neck so it hangs on your chest.

▶ Put on your headdress.

▶ You are ready to enter the Tabernacle!

▶ Slowly walk across the room in your new outfit. Pretend to walk through the tent flap of the Tabernacle. Lift your arms in the air, and light the Menorah. Reach out your hands to accept a gift from the Israelites and carry it into the Tabernacle. How do you feel?

You'll Need
- a towel
- breastplate and headdress (from the MAKE activities above)
- masking tape or string

How do you feel different when you dress up in a costume, special clothing, or uniform?

CHAPTER 21

The Golden Calf Surprise

Exodus 30:11–34:35 • *Parashat Ki Tisa* • כִּי תִשָּׂא

Collect building materials, construct the Golden Calf,
and act out the moment Moses discovered what the
Israelites did while he was up on the mountain.

Have you ever been frustrated while you waited for something to happen?

While Moses was inside the cloud on top of Mount Sinai, the Israelites waited. And waited. And waited. "What if Moses never comes back? What if he doesn't bring back any instructions from God?" they worried. They started to doubt everything.

As they got more and more nervous, they decided they needed to build a new god. "Aaron, help us make a new god to lead us!" they pleaded.

Aaron wondered if the people were right. "Gather all of your gold, and bring it to me," Aaron declared.

The Israelites collected all their shiny gold, and Aaron burned it down, sculpting it into a statue of a golden calf. "This golden cow will be our new god!" Aaron said.

The Israelites cheered! They threw a wild party and celebrated by dancing around the statue all night. They were singing so loudly that they didn't notice Moses running down from the top of the mountain. "What do you think you are doing?!" Moses yelled down from the path, holding the two stone tablets with the Ten Commandments carved on them.

Moses couldn't believe what he saw. Why weren't the people more patient? And his own brother leading them in making this mistake? Moses was so angry that the people had lost faith while he was gone, he threw the tablets to the ground, breaking them into pieces.

"Moses . . . we're so sorry. We don't know what we were thinking!" they cried.

"We were nervous that you still hadn't come back, and things just got out of hand," Aaron said, staring at their silly golden statue.

Moses went back up the mountain to get a new set of tablets. "Just be patient. I'll be back soon!" Moses warned.

This time, the Israelites knew that they just needed to wait and he would come back.

Imagine Imagine yourself getting so tired of waiting for Moses that you build a new god out of gold!

▶ What do you think you would have done if you were feeling worried that Moses wouldn't return?

▶ Why do you think Aaron helped the people build the Golden Calf? How do you think Aaron felt when he saw his brother Moses coming back down the mountain?

Have you ever had trouble waiting for something? Were you patient, waiting until the right time, or did you try to do it earlier?

▶ What would you have said to Moses after he broke the stone tablets?

 Make Use your materials and your creativity to construct your version of the Golden Calf (and destroy it in the next activity!).

▶ Look through all of your toys, and collect all of your building materials (for example, plastic building blocks) that are the color yellow or orange to represent the gold pieces the Israelites gathered.

You'll Need

• yellow and orange building materials

▶ Once you've collected all of them, put them in one big container.

▶ Think about the shape of a cow. What are the different parts of its body?

▶ See if you can make a cow statue using your yellow and orange building materials.

▶ Build the legs first, then the body, then the head.

▶ Use your imagination and experiment with different ways to construct your cow using all of the yellow and orange materials you gathered. See if you can use all of the pieces you collected in your statue's design.

What do you do to pass the time while you are waiting for something to happen?

▶ You'll knock down this statue in the next activity.

Play **Act out the moment when Moses returned to see the Israelites dancing around the Golden Calf.**

▶ Decide who will play the Israelites and who will play Moses.

▶ The Israelites should dance and sing in a circle around the Golden Calf.

▶ Moses should walk in from the other room holding the Ten Commandments. Moses sees the Golden Calf, makes a surprised and then angry face, and says, "How could you?!" He throws the Ten Commandments tablets to the ground.

▶ The Israelites say, "I'm so sorry! I didn't think you would come back!"

▶ They knock down and destroy the Golden Calf statue.

▶ Moses turns around and walks back to the mountain.

▶ Once you act out this scene, rebuild your Golden Calf statue, and switch roles so that everyone gets a chance to play Moses and the Israelites.

> **You'll Need**
> • your Golden Calf (from the MAKE activity on page 83)
> • your cardboard Ten Commandments (from the MAKE activity on page 74).

> How do you greet someone when they get back after being away for a while?

CHAPTER 22

Time for the Tabernacle

Exodus 35:1–38:20 • *Parashat Vayakheil* • וַיַּקְהֵל

Practice your building skills, create the special curtain in the Tabernacle, and keep the Ten Commandments safe.

Have you ever worked on a team to build something together?

"Gather around everyone, it's time to build!" Bezalel heard Moses say from the middle of the campsite as he returned from the mountain, this time with a new set of tablets.

As Moses described a brand-new construction project that would take creativity and crafting, Bezalel nearly jumped in the air. "This is my chance!" he thought. Bezalel loved to build and create, and he was really good at putting things together. He raised his hand and said, "I can help!"

Bezalel became the chief builder of the Tabernacle (called the *Mishkan* in Hebrew), a portable temple that would travel with the Israelites wherever they went in the wilderness. The Tabernacle would be a place to say prayers, sing songs, and bring gifts of thanks. "We'll need all kinds of stuff," Bezalel shared, his mind already planning how to build the temple using the instructions from God. "Bring your silver, stones, colorful fabric, and goat hair. We're going to need all of it. Everyone can play a part!"

The Israelites took this invitation to heart. They searched across the camp and gathered all of their precious materials for the project. "Here you go, Bezalel!" they said as they delivered their materials. Everyone wanted to help and be a part of building the Tabernacle in their own way.

Bezalel's team worked together day and night to create the Tabernacle, sharing ideas to make something beautiful. They rested each seventh day for Shabbat. They worked together to create the poles, the curtains, and the gates. Finally, Bezalel and his team built the Ark, where the Ten Commandments were kept safe, and put it inside the Holy of Holies—the room in the Tabernacle where the Ark would stand.

"This is just right," Bezalel thought as he hammered the final piece in place on the Ark. "Great work, everyone!"

Imagine Imagine yourself being on the team that helps to build the Tabernacle in the wilderness.

▶ What do you imagine the Tabernacle looked like? What kinds of spaces would they need to say prayers, sing songs, and bring gifts of thanks?

▶ What kinds of special materials do you think the people brought to build the Tabernacle? What material would you bring?

▶ How do builders work together to create something?

> What is the most exciting thing you have built or constructed on your own?

 **Make** Create your own special place to keep the Ten Commandments safe.

▶ Find a table to put at the center of your Tabernacle.

▶ Around the table, create a fence around your Tabernacle using masking tape on the floor.

▶ Put the bedsheet over the table, imagining that this is the curtain called the *parochet* that stands in front of the holiest place in the Tabernacle.

▶ Find a special container to use as your Ark to keep the cardboard Ten Commandments safe.

You'll Need
• a table
• masking tape
• a bedsheet
• a container
• cardboard Ten Commandments (from the MAKE activity in chapter 18)

▶ Take the container with the Ten Commandments, and put it under the table behind the curtain.

▶ Sit under the table, imagining that you are in the Holy of Holies in the Tabernacle.

> What is your favorite material you like to use to create something?

Explore Create your own designs, and then build them out of physical materials.

▶ Gather building materials you would like to use. You can use blocks, plastic building bricks, magnetic tiles, or another building material.

▶ Decide who will be the architect and who will be the builder.

▶ The architect, using the pen and paper, draws a shape that they imagine being built from the chosen materials.

▶ When the architect is done, they hand the drawing (or the "blueprint") to the builder.

> **You'll Need**
> • building materials
> • paper
> • a pen

▶ The builder uses the materials to create a 3D version of the shape drawn on the piece of paper.

▶ When you are done, switch roles so that everyone has a chance to both design and build.

▶ For younger players, create a blueprint with only two or three shapes. For older players, try to create more difficult and imaginative shapes as you go, and challenge yourselves to construct them.

> Do you prefer being the architect or the builder? Why?

CHAPTER 23

The Cloud Comes Down to Rest

Exodus 38:21–40:38 • *Parashat P'kudei* • פְקוּדֵי

Create your own edible Tabernacle, and fill it with a divine cloud (of popcorn)!

Have you worked really hard on a project? What did you do when you finished? Did you rest?

"Now it's time for us to get ready to use this beautiful Tabernacle," said Aaron, as he looked out at the beautiful place that Bezalel and his team had built in the middle of the camp. Every part was exactly where it needed to be, and the entire camp was excited to see the Tabernacle standing tall.

Bezalel's team brought all of the pieces of Aaron's uniform, which they had made exactly to the instructions God provided. Aaron and his sons put on each piece of their uniform and prepared to begin their work in the Tabernacle. "You look great, brother," Moses said. "I think we're ready."

As the sun came up, the Israelites noticed something mysterious in the sky. A cloud glided down and hovered over the Tabernacle. "What is that?" they asked, frozen in place.

"Don't be afraid. That cloud means that God has come to rest inside of the Tabernacle you built," Moses said.

Bezalel beamed, proud of the work that the whole team had accomplished. "We've come a long way since Egypt," Aaron chimed in. "Even though we may feel like we're lost in the wilderness, now that we have the Tabernacle we'll always feel at home, wherever we go."

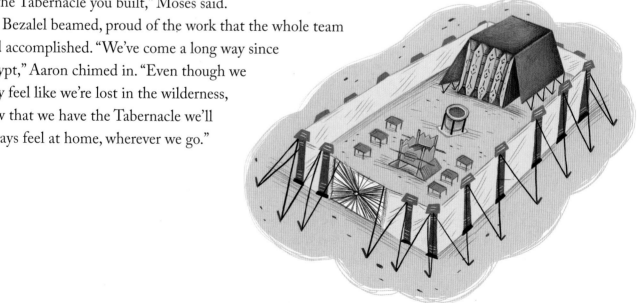

Imagine Imagine yourself seeing the cloud hovering over the Tabernacle after you finished building.

▶ How would you feel if you were one of the Israelites who just finished the project of creating the Tabernacle?

▶ How would you feel if you were one of the *kohanim* and you had the responsibility of working in the Tabernacle for all of the Israelite people?

> Have you ever finished a big project? How did it feel?

 **Make** Use the materials and your creativity to construct an edible Tabernacle.

▶ Take a look at the image on the previous page depicting the Tabernacle. What do you notice about the structure? What are the different parts? What shapes do you see? What colors and textures do you see?

▶ On your baking sheet, spread a layer of decorating icing as a floor.

You'll Need:
- a baking sheet
- a box of large graham crackers
- decorating icing
- sprinkles
- candy to decorate (gumdrops, etc.)
- candy melts
- pretzel rods

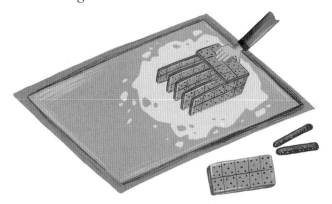

▶ On top of the icing, place five graham crackers horizontally in a row to be the entrance columns.

▶ Place a gumdrop or other candy in the middle row for the ark.

▶ Spread icing on two graham crackers and attach them across the top of the columns. Add two more on either side on a diagonal leaning against the structure. (See reference image.) These four graham crackers will act as the tent covering.

▶ Melt down the candy melts, and spread out the mixture on top of the graham cracker tent covering. Spread sprinkles over the top to decorate it.

> Did you ever work really hard building or making something that is temporary (that you knew wouldn't last a long time)?

▶ Break a graham cracker into pieces that will fit between your columns. Decorate them with icing and candy. Attach them in between the columns as part of the facade.

▶ Spread a rectangle of icing around the structure.

▶ Lay down pretzel rods in the icing as the fence perimeter around the Tabernacle. Add a rectangle of graham crackers as the fence.

Play Act out the moment when the cloud comes to rest over the Tabernacle.

▶ Take a big handful of popcorn in your hand. Pretend it is a big cloud.

You'll Need
• your edible Tabernacle (from the MAKE activity above) • popcorn

▶ Make the sound effect of a moving cloud (perhaps the sound of wind blowing).

▶ Slowly move your "cloud" over the Tabernacle.

▶ Drop the popcorn on top of the whole structure, like the cloud hovering over the Tabernacle.

Where do you gather with other people in a big group? How does it feel to all be together there?

Completing Exodus
A Celebration Ritual

You've just finished the book of Exodus! You traveled with the Israelites from slavery to freedom and all the way to Mount Sinai to get the Ten Commandments. Whew! Good work. Let's mark this milestone together.

Unroll the Scroll

Imagine that you are the big scroll of the Torah. Stand really tall, with your arms at your sides. On the count of three, do *two* giant spins to pretend that you are unrolling the scroll past Genesis and Exodus to the next section of the Torah. One, two, three, spin!

Shout a Cheer

Say together in Hebrew, English, or both:

"Chazak, chazak, v'nit'chazeik!"

"Be strong, be strong, and we'll be strong together!"

You can say these words together, or come up with your own cheer for Exodus. (For example, "We're free! We're free! Let's celebrate—you and me!")

Celebrate

Have a party to celebrate everything you've learned and explored. Dance like Miriam, lift your arms into the air like Moses, or make a beautiful craft like Bezalel. Plan how you want to mark the moment together, and celebrate your own way!

LEVITICUS

BECOMING A PEOPLE OF OUR OWN

Learn with the Israelites as Moses teaches them all the lessons he brought back from the top of Mount Sinai. No longer slaves to Pharaoh in Egypt, the Israelites must figure out what it means to be free as they grow as a people. What do they believe in? How do they want to treat each other and the world around them? Before they settle in a land of their own, they'll need to figure out who they want to be as a nation.

As you join them in building a community, you'll smell the spices used in the traveling Tabernacle in the wilderness, tend to the Israelites who get sick along the journey, and explore what it means to take care of the land we live on.

CHAPTER 24

Bring Your Best Offering

Leviticus 1:1–5:26 • *Parashat Vayikra* • וַיִּקְרָא

Explore the idea of bringing offerings, make an offering of love, and test your sense of smell.

How do you show you are sorry? How do you show you are grateful?

Soon after the Tabernacle was built, Moses heard a voice coming from inside the tent. "Moses, you need to teach the Israelites how to use the Tabernacle. They can bring Me offerings here for many different reasons," God told Moses.

"What is an offering?" Moses asked. God told Moses that the Israelites should bring different gifts called "offerings" to the Tabernacle.

"When should they bring offerings?" Moses wondered. God explained that the Israelites could bring their offerings to the entrance of the Tabernacle when they needed to apologize for something they had done wrong or if they wanted to say thank you for something great that had happened to them.

Moses went back to the Israelites and shared everything he learned. "What can we bring as an offering?" asked one Israelite.

"What do we have that would be special enough to bring?" asked another.

Moses told the Israelites to bring animals, grains, breads, and other types of food to the Tabernacle as their offering gifts. They should also bring spices to burn and create sweet smells. Soon, Aaron and his sons would be there to help collect the gifts and bring them into the tent. As the Israelites began to prepare their gifts and new smells filled the air around the camp, Moses saw that the Tabernacle was beginning to buzz with the hustle and bustle of Israelites bringing offerings to God, just as he imagined it would.

Imagine Imagine yourself bringing offerings to the Tabernacle.

▶ What would you bring to the Tabernacle as an offering?

▶ Why do you think it was important for the Israelites to have a way to apologize when they did something they felt bad about or to show thanks when they had something to feel grateful for?

▶ How do you think they felt after visiting the Tabernacle?

> What do you do to thank someone? How do you show you are sorry?

 Explore Use your sense of smell to explore different spices.

▶ One person covers their eyes with a bandana.

▶ The other person raises the first spice to the smeller's nose while announcing, "This is spice number 1."

▶ Repeat this step with the second and third spice.

▶ The smeller takes a whiff of each spice and shares their favorite based on the smell.

▶ Take off the bandana. Look at the spices and notice the colors and textures of the ones you ranked higher and lower. Identify the names of each of the spices.

▶ In a small bowl, experiment with mixing two different spices together, and try to make the most pleasing combination possible.

▶ Talk about which of the spices you'd use for a sweet-smelling offering, which smell was least pleasing, and which smell was most surprising.

You'll Need
- a bandana
- 3 different spices
- a small bowl

 **Make** Use the materials and your creativity to create a special gift, your offering, for someone else.

▶ Think about someone to whom you want to offer love, gratitude, and appreciation. It can be a family member, a teacher, a friend, or even a pet. (Keep your offering a secret from them until it is done!)

▶ Design a special card as your offering. Color a picture on the front, and write a loving message on the inside.

You'll Need
- construction paper
- crayons

Play Deliver your offering to the Tabernacle.

▶ Once your message is complete, the deliverer can ask the recipient to sit in a chair across the room.

> **You'll Need**
> - offering card (from the MAKE activity above)
> - a bedsheet

> Why is it important to show how we feel with actions in addition to our words?

▶ The recipient can hold up the bedsheet as a curtain, imagining this is the entrance to the Tabernacle.

▶ The deliverer can walk across the room and open the curtain to present the offering to the recipient, imagining they brought it to the Tabernacle.

For Groups:

You can assign each person a recipient, so that everyone will create an offering and receive one too. Alternatively, everyone can design an offering with a message of love for the whole group. Split the group in half, so that everyone can take turns delivering and receiving the offering.

CHAPTER 25

Keep the Fire Burning Bright

Leviticus 6:1–8:36 • *Parashat Tzav* • צו

Imagine you are one of the *kohanim* (priests) in the Tabernacle, and use flour and oil to create a tasty meal offering.

Have you ever participated in a ceremony?

The Israelites looked up at the Tabernacle, the portable temple that they built using the instructions that God gave them. "It's time to get the Tabernacle up and running!" Aaron said.

Aaron and his sons had prepared for their important jobs as the *kohanim*, the special team that would take care of the Tabernacle for the rest of the people. The day of the big ceremony to officially open the Tabernacle arrived, and Aaron had butterflies in his stomach. "Am I ready?" he asked his wife, Elisheva.

"Of course, you're ready," she said. "Has there ever been a more joyous day? I am so proud of you and our sons."

Aaron took a deep breath and put on his uniform—a shiny plate with stones across his chest, a robe around his waist, and a headdress on his head.

Elisheva watched with tears in her eyes. She said, "You look wonderful."

Aaron looked at his reflection, wearing this very fancy uniform, and he felt ready to begin. "Now, it's time to fill the Tabernacle with light," he said.

Aaron and his sons made sure that the fire in the Tabernacle burned brightly day and night. They also accepted the offerings that the Israelites brought, including the animals, spices, and bread made from oil and flour. The ceremony lasted for seven days. For that whole time, Aaron and his sons stayed inside the Tabernacle learning their new jobs.

"Good work, everyone," Aaron said. He smiled at his sons, proud that they would keep the Tabernacle running no matter where their travels took them in the wilderness.

Imagine Imagine yourself working alongside Aaron and his sons in the Tabernacle.

▶ How do you think Aaron felt putting on his uniform for the first time?

▶ How do you think you would feel if you were one of the *kohanim*, standing in front of the Tabernacle and starting this special job in front of the whole community?

▶ How would you work with the rest of your family as a team to keep the fire burning all the time? How might you take turns to make sure the light never went out?

> Have you ever needed to learn how to do a specific activity or job? Who taught you how to do it? How long did it take you to learn the new skill?

 Make Make a meal offering from flour and oil, like the *kohanim*.

This activity involves cooking, and it will require some additional support from a grown-up.

▶ In a mixing bowl, slowly add half the flour to the room-temperature water.

▶ Add 1 tablespoon of olive oil once half of the flour is mixed.

▶ Add the rest of the flour, and mix it all together.

▶ Once you have a ball of dough, knead on a lightly floured wooden board or baking sheet for a few minutes.

▶ Cover with plastic wrap, and let the dough rest for about twenty minutes at room temperature.

▶ Divide the dough into three balls, and roll out each ball to a six-inch round disk.

You'll Need
• a mixing bowl
• ½ cup of water
• 1¼ cups of flour
• 1 tablespoon of oil
• wooden board or baking sheet
• plastic wrap
• rolling pin
• a stovetop
• a large grill pan, cast-iron skillet, or nonstick pan

▶ Heat a large grill pan, cast-iron skillet, or nonstick pan over medium-high heat.

▶ Add the dough disks and cook for about one to two minutes on each side.

▶ Like an ancient Israelite priest, eat your tasty meal offering!

> Have you ever worked together on a project with your family? What jobs did everyone have? What did you create together?

Play Act out the ceremony of becoming a *kohein*.

▶ Find the priestly uniform that you made in chapter 20. If you no longer have it, go back to the instructions in chapter 20 to create a new one.

▶ Create a special ceremony to put on your *kohein* uniform. Decide who will be Moses and who will be Aaron.

▶ Moses can wrap the towel around the waist of Aaron, like a tunic.

▶ Moses can put the breastplate around Aaron's neck.

▶ Moses can put the headdress on Aaron. How do you think Aaron feels when Moses puts the headdress on him? Show this with your facial expression and movements.

> **You'll Need**
> - a towel
> - breastplate and headdress (from the MAKE activities in chapter 20)
> - masking tape or string
> - a bedsheet

▶ Moses can hold up a bedsheet to be the opening of the Tabernacle.

▶ Aaron can walk across the room and go behind the sheet, imagining the entrance to the Tabernacle.

▶ Now switch roles so that everyone gets a chance to play Moses and Aaron.

For Groups:

With multiple players, you can have half of the group play Moses and half of the group play Aaron. You can also start with two people acting out the scene while the rest of the group watches as the audience. Take turns playing each of the roles.

> Have you ever watched a family member or friend receive a big honor, like a graduation ceremony or a trophy after a game? How did watching them make you feel? What did you say to them afterward?

CHAPTER 26

Learning to Eat by Land and Sea

Leviticus 9:1–11:47 • *Parashat Sh'mini* • שְׁמִינִי

Explore the land and sea creatures that the Israelites were allowed to eat for food, and think about the food you eat.

What foods do you love to eat, and which foods would you never eat?

Aaron and his sons stayed in the Tabernacle for seven days. Finally, the eighth day arrived. Aaron led the way as all the other *kohanim* (priests) walked out of the tent of the Tabernacle and into the sunlight.

All of the Israelites gathered in front of the Tabernacle to see them. Aaron lifted his hands out toward the people and gave them a blessing. Suddenly, the people saw a giant fire light up in front of the Tabernacle. "God has come to rest here with us," Aaron said. "We created a beautiful place here in the wilderness, and you all played a part in making it feel like a home."

Now that the Tabernacle was ready, the Israelites brought gifts to God, including the best of their animals. These animals stayed at the Tabernacle, but the Israelites had more animals back at their tents. They wondered if they were allowed to cook and eat any of these animals with their families. "I learned about this from God on the mountain," Moses said. "I'll teach you the new rules for which animals we can eat and which animals we can't eat."

Moses explained there were different clues to look for if the animal lived on land or in the sea.

"If a land animal has a split in its hooves and it chews its food again and again, it is okay to eat, like cows and sheep," he explained. "If a fish has fins and scales along its body, it is okay to eat."

These new instructions about eating made the Israelites think about the food they put in their bodies in a whole new way. All that talk of food also made them hungry, especially for the foods they couldn't find while they were camping in the wilderness!

Note: Many children and families have their own practices around dietary restrictions, including kosher, vegan, or gluten-free, to name a few. You can use this introduction to the concept of kosher to explore a larger conversation about the decisions we make about food.

Imagine **Imagine yourself exploring the land and searching the sea for all the different animals that the Israelites were allowed to eat.**

▶ How do you think the Israelites felt about getting instructions for what to eat and not eat?

▶ What food would you miss most if you were on a journey through the wilderness with the Israelites?

▶ Which animals do you think they found while traveling in the desert?

> What are your favorite foods to eat? What foods does your family love to eat together?

 Make Create a fish that has fins and scales!

▶ Photocopy or trace and cut out the Fish Template on page 103.

▶ Cut out four small triangles (one to two inches high) from the construction paper.

▶ Tape the triangles to your fish to add fins on the top and bottom and a tail at the back.

▶ Use dot stickers to create scales on the fish body.

> **You'll Need**
> • Fish Template (page 103)
> • construction paper
> • scissors
> • tape
> • dot stickers

> Why is it important to think about the choices we make about food?

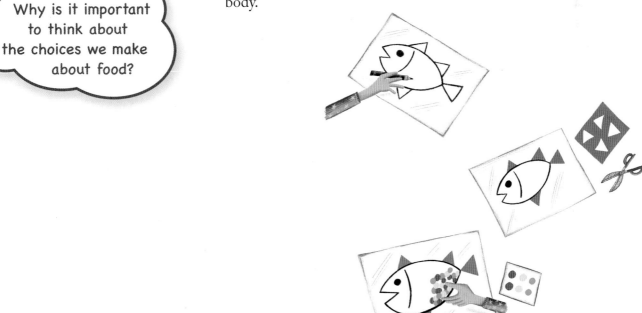

Play Do animal-shape yoga as you move your body to create the shapes of the animals that the Israelites were allowed to eat.

▶ Use the images provided as a guide to create the yoga pose representing each of the following kosher animals:

▶ **Cow:** Get down on all fours, with your knees under your hips and your wrists under your shoulders. Drop your belly, arch your back, and raise your eyes to look at the ceiling.

▶ **Chicken:** Squat down with your tailbone between your ankles, your palms pressed together, and your elbows against your knees.

> How do you and your family decide what to eat or not eat? Do you have rules about which foods to eat?

▶ **Fish:** Lie flat on your back. Bring your arms to your sides. Lift your upper body off the ground while resting your weight on your forearms and hips. Keep your head and your lower body on the floor.

Cow   Chicken   Fish

Fish Template

Follow the instructions to create a fish in the MAKE activity on page 101.

CHAPTER 27

See Spot, Run!

Leviticus 12:1–13:59 • *Parashat Tazri'a* • תַזְרִיעַ

**Explore the mysterious *tzara'at* rash, become a *kohein*
to protect the Israelites, and think about what it means
to take care of your friends through sickness.**

Have you ever stayed away from other people while you were sick?

One morning, an Israelite was taking a bath when she noticed her reflection in the water. Her skin was covered in a patchy colorful rash! "What is this? And what should I do to take care of it?" she wondered.

While in the wilderness, the Israelites sometimes got a mysterious sickness called *tzara'at*. The Israelite with the rash went straight to Aaron for help. "Aaron, do I have *tzara'at*? What do I do?" she said, trying not to panic.

"Don't worry," he said. "While you are sick, let's set you up in a tent just outside the campsite, so that you have a quiet place to rest up and feel better."

She left the camp right away, setting up a tent just outside of the camp. In the distance, she could see all of her friends. She couldn't wait until she was better so that she could go back and play with them. Aaron visited her often and took care of her. "How are you feeling today?" he asked as he checked on her symptoms.

After seven days, she saw that her rash was gone.

"It looks like you are back to yourself!" Aaron said.

They walked back to camp together, and the Israelite was happy to rejoin the community again. "Thanks for taking care of me," she said to Aaron.

The people knew that whenever they came down with *tzara'at*, Aaron and the *kohanim* could help take care of them.

Imagine **Imagine yourself as a *kohein* taking care of a sick Israelite.**

▶ How do you think the Israelites felt when they saw they had *tzara'at* on their skin?

▶ How do you think the *kohein* could help make the person feel better?

▶ What do you think the community could do to make the sick person feel included even when they had to quarantine outside of the camp?

> Who takes care of you when you get sick?

 Make **Use stickers, paper, and your own face to explore the mysterious *tzara'at*.**

▶ Draw the shape of a face on a piece of paper.

▶ Imagine what *tzara'at*, a mysterious skin rash that the Israelites got while in the wilderness, might look like.

▶ Draw and design what you imagine it looks like on the piece of paper.

You'll Need
• paper
• markers
• colorful dot stickers
• a mirror

▶ Use your own face to explore *tzara'at*. Take turns putting colorful dot stickers on each other's face, imagining that they are a *tzara'at* skin rash.

▶ Go to the mirror and take a look at your *tzara'at*.

▶ Make silly faces in the mirror, imagining how the Israelites felt when they saw the *tzara'at* on their skin!

> What do you do when you are home sick?

Explore Your skin is the largest organ of your body. It helps you sense the world around you. Think about your skin and explore the way different textures make you feel.

▶ One person can be the explorer, and one person can be the guide.

▶ The explorer covers their face with the bandana or cloth. Make sure it totally covers the eyes so that the explorer can't see anything.

▶ The guide can introduce the different materials gently on different parts of the skin of the explorer (on their arm, face, or leg), one at a time.

▶ After each object or material, ask the explorer to describe how it made them feel (for example, it was cold or hot, bumpy or smooth).

▶ Switch roles so that each person has a chance to be the explorer and the guide.

You'll Need
- a bandana or cloth
- ice cube
- cotton balls
- soft fabric
- sandpaper
- a sponge wet with warm water
- aluminum foil

 Play Become a *kohein* and visit a sick Israelite.

▶ Take a stuffed animal and use the dot stickers to create *tzara'at* on their skin or fur.

▶ Use the pillows, bedsheet, and chairs to create a tent for your stuffed animal Israelite outside of the camp.

You'll Need
- stuffed animal
- dot stickers
- pillows
- a bedsheet
- chairs

▶ Pretend to be the *kohein* coming to give the Israelite an examination. Check their skin, ask how they are doing, and make sure they are comfortable.

> How does a community make sure that people who are sick are able to get better?

▶ Pretend to return several times. When the *kohein* feels like the *tzara'at* is going away (you can remove a sticker at a time), the Israelite can come back to the main camp and be reunited with the rest of the people.

For Groups

With multiple players, you can have everyone take care of their own stuffed animal or work in groups to visit the sick Israelite.

CHAPTER 28

A Plague on My House

Leviticus 14:1–15:33 • *Parashat M'tzora* • מְצֹרָע

**Explore the mysterious *tzara'at* on the walls of a house, become
a *kohein* to inspect the houses of the Israelites, and think
about the ways we take care of the places where we live.**

How do you take care of the place where you live?

"Wait a minute . . . our houses can get sick too?" an Israelite asked in disbelief in the middle of one of Moses's lessons for the people. Moses taught them that the mysterious sickness called *tzara'at* not only popped up on a person's skin, but could also appear on the walls of the houses they would live in when they settled in the land of Canaan. Even though they were still in the middle of the wilderness, God's instructions prepared them for what life would be like when they finally settled in a permanent home.

"How will we know that the house is sick?" asked the Israelite, trying to imagine what it might look like.

Moses explained that the house would be covered in red and green streaks that spread deep into the walls.

"What will we do?! I know we live only in tents now, but I want to be ready when we finally live in houses again!" the Israelite said.

"Don't worry, we have a plan," Moses said. "When a house becomes sick with *tzara'at*, the *kohanim* will visit to look at it and remove it."

The Israelite went back to his tent that night, thinking about how he couldn't wait to take care of a real house once they finally made it to Canaan. "One day I'll leave this tent," he thought as he went to sleep. "But I hope my walls never turn red and green."

 **Imagine** **Imagine yourself as a *kohein* inspecting a house with *tzara'at* on the walls.**

▶ How do you think the Israelites felt when they saw they had *tzara'at* on the walls of their house?

▶ How do you think the *kohein* would get rid of the green or red streaks that appeared on the house walls?

▶ What do you think the community could do to support the Israelites who needed to rebuild their houses because of the *tzara'at*?

> How do you take care of your house?

 Explore **Make mold grow to imagine what *tzara'at* looked like!**

▶ Spray water onto a piece of bread.

▶ Put it into a sealed bag. Make sure the bag is tightly closed.

▶ Put the bag in a drawer away from the light. (Mold grows faster in the dark!)

You'll Need
• bread
• water
• a sealable plastic bag

> Why is it important to clean up and care for the place where you live?

▶ Check on it in a week—but don't open the bag! Has it grown mold? Take a look at the splotch on the bread as a way to imagine *tzara'at* growing on a house wall.

▶ Make sure to throw away the moldy bread.

Play **Become a *kohein* and inspect the house for *tzara'at*.**

▶ To prepare, one person takes a few sheets of construction paper and cuts them into splotchy shapes.

▶ Tape them up around the walls, and turn down the lights.

▶ Now, the other person imagines they are the *kohein*, tasked with inspecting the house for *tzara'at*.

▶ The inspector takes a flashlight and a spatula and searches the walls to see if they can find any green or red splotches.

▶ When they find one, they try to remove it using the spatula without touching the splotch with their hands.

▶ The inspector should try to find all of the *tzara'at* in the house and remove it.

▶ Put the splotchy shapes back up on the walls. Switch roles and act out the scene again.

You'll Need
- red and green construction paper
- scissors
- tape
- a flashlight
- a spatula

> Who do you call to help if your house needs fixing?

CHAPTER 29

Take It Away, Goat!

Leviticus 16:1–18:30 • *Parashat Acharei Mot* • אַחֲרֵי מוֹת

Discover the rituals of Yom Kippur, send your regrets away with the scapegoat, and think about how we can learn from our mistakes.

Have you ever said you were sorry for a mistake you made?

It was the morning of Yom Kippur in the middle of the wilderness, and an Israelite girl felt nervous. She thought about the year that had passed, and she remembered mean things she had said to her friends in the camp. "How can I leave these mistakes behind and make them right from now on?" she wondered.

"Today we say we're sorry to God and to each other for the mistakes we made this year," she heard Aaron say from the center of the campsite, as if he was speaking to her inner thoughts. "Together, we think about ways we can become our best selves in the future."

As the Israelite joined the rest of the camp for the annual ceremony, she saw Aaron and the *kohanim* walking with one very special goat. Aaron raised his hands over the goat's head and shared all of the Israelites' mistakes in front of the chosen goat. The girl imagined that this goat held each of her mistakes on its back. "It's time to send them away as we move into the new year," Aaron said.

She watched as the goat was sent away on a big journey into the wilderness, carrying all the mistakes away so that the Israelites could begin a new year with a clean slate. The Israelite girl knew she still needed to apologize to her friends for saying mean things, but the goat was a good start. The girl took a deep breath and walked back to her tent, feeling lighter and filled with hope for the new year.

 **Imagine** Imagine yourself sharing your mistakes with your community and sending the goat into the wilderness.

▶ Why do you think it was important for the Israelites to have a day once a year to think about the mistakes they wanted to apologize for?

▶ How do you think the Israelites felt after watching the goat walk into the wilderness?

▶ What do you think the Israelite girl did after seeing the goat journey into the wilderness? Do you think she changed her behavior in any way?

> How do you show you are sorry when you've done something wrong?

 Make Make your own miniature goat, and fill it with things you want to change.

▶ Photocopy or trace, color, and cut out the Goat Face and Tail Template (page 113).

▶ Attach the goat face to one side of the tissue box and the tail to the opposite side.

You'll Need

● Goat Face and Tail Template (page 113)
● crayons or markers
● an empty tissue box
● scissors
● tape
● paper

▶ Think about things you've done that you want to change or do differently in the future. Write or draw them on pieces of paper and put them into your goat box.

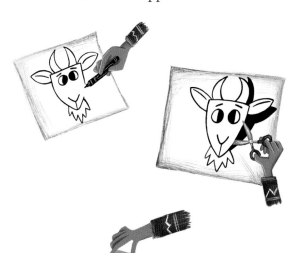

Tip: Keep this box and add ideas to it whenever you do something you want to change.

Play   ## Become the goat sent into the wilderness.

▶ Cut strips of construction paper to become a band around your head. Measure the right length for your head, and then staple the strips together.

▶ Draw two goat ears on a separate sheet of paper. Color and attach the goat ears to the front of the band.

▶ Put the band on your head.

▶ Get on the floor and create the shape of a goat with your body.

▶ Use the blankets or sheets to represent all of the mistakes that the Israelites are sending away with the goat into the wilderness. Put the blankets or sheets on your back.

▶ Try walking away into the "wilderness" across the room, carrying this load on your back. How does it feel to carry away all of the "mistakes" on your back?

> **You'll Need**
> • construction paper
> • scissors
> • stapler or tape
> • blankets or sheets

> Does saying you're sorry make the hurt you've caused go away? What else can you do besides using your words?

For Groups:

With multiple players, you can have half the group be the goat and half the group put all of the blankets and sheets on top of the goats to send them away. Alternatively, you can ask one child to be the goat while the rest of the group plays the Israelites.

Goat Face and Tail Template

Attach the goat face to one side of a tissue box and the tail to the opposite side. Follow the instructions in the MAKE activity.

CHAPTER 30

Walk in Their Shoes

Leviticus 19:1–20:27 • *Parashat K'doshim* • קְדֹשִׁים

Explore the way you can treat someone else the way you want to be treated, and take a walk in each other's shoes.

How do you honor the people who love and take care of you?

Moses spent each day teaching the Israelites lessons that he learned while on top of Mount Sinai. "These commandments, called *mitzvot*, will give you a plan for how to be a good person—for yourself and for your community," Moses said to the people.

"Don't forget about the people who raise you, take care of you, and love you. You need to respect and honor them," Moses said.

That night, an Israelite went home to his tent and cleaned up before his parents came home. He fed the animals, washed the clothing, and cleaned the floor. When his parents came home, they couldn't believe that all of the chores were done. "You take a rest tonight," he said to them. "Thank you for everything you do to take care of me. I love you!"

Moses also shared one of the most important lessons he learned: love your fellow person just as you love yourself, and treat other people the way you want to be treated.

The next day, another Israelite was drinking a big jug of water to cool off from the heat. She looked up and noticed that her friend was sweating in the hot sun. "Your cheeks are all red, and you look so tired. Here, take my water to drink," the Israelite said as she handed the jug to her friend. "Even though I'm feeling hot, I think you need it more than I do."

Moses smiled as he noticed the ways that the Israelites used God's lessons all throughout the camp.

 **Imagine yourself learning these important lessons while traveling through the desert with the Israelites.**

▶ Why do you think it was important for the Israelites to receive a bunch of commandments on how to be good people after they left Egypt?

▶ What does it mean to "love your fellow person just as you love yourself"? How do you think the Israelites could show their friends that they cared about them just as much as they cared about themselves?

▶ Many people believe that "love your fellow person just as you love yourself" is the most important lesson of all. Why do you think many people feel this way? Do you agree?

 Make a treat for someone as you learn about treating others the way you want to be treated.

▶ Interview a friend or family member about what they like. Ask them questions like:

> **You'll Need**
> • paper
> • crayons or markers
> • other craft supplies as needed

  • What is your favorite food?

  • What is your favorite color?

  • What is your favorite place to visit?

  • What is your favorite game to play?

  • How do you like other people to treat you?

▶ Draw pictures showing the things you learned about them to hang up as party decorations.

▶ Celebrate the person you interviewed by using their answers as inspiration. Play their favorite game, wear their favorite color, and eat their favorite food. Make the day all about them!

▶ If you are playing with a group, either pair up to interview each other, or choose a special guest to interview all together.

> Why do you think it is important to treat other people the way you want to be treated?

Play Switch places and pretend play so that kids can feel what it's like to be grown-ups, and grown-ups can remember what it's like to be a kid.

▶ Choose some pieces of clothing that can help you dress up as each other, and imagine that you are the other person (grown-up as kid, and kid as grown-up).

> **You'll Need**
> • dress-up costumes
> • household items

▶ Think about some of the things that the grown-up does that the kid doesn't do. (For example, if you are playing at home, you can pretend to cook dinner or go to work. If you are playing at school, you can pretend to lead the class and give instructions to the room.)

▶ Think about some of the things that the kid does that the grown-up doesn't do. (For example, if you are playing at home, you can explore playing with toys and jumping in the mud. If you are playing at school, you can explore sitting at a child's table or playing with a doll.)

> How did pretending to be the other person make you appreciate what it is like to be them? Why is it important to respect the grown-ups or kids in your life?

▶ Take turns acting out different parts of the day as if you were the other person.

▶ What was it like to be the grown-up? What was it like to be the kid? What did you learn about the other person?

For Groups:

With multiple players, ask all of the children to choose a grown-up to pretend to be. Within a larger family, different members of the family can pretend to be other members of the family regardless of age. In a classroom, students can take turns pretending to be the teacher, or all of the students can try it at the same time.

CHAPTER 31

Holiday Time

Leviticus 21:1–24:23 • *Parashat Emor* • אֱמוֹר

Learn about some of the Jewish holidays that we celebrate, and explore the counting of the omer!

How do holidays help us remember stories from the past?

The days became weeks, and the weeks became months as the Israelites traveled through the wilderness. One season blended into the next. God told Moses to give the Israelites a calendar of holidays to celebrate all together.

"These are the special days that we will celebrate as a community," Moses told the people. "They will mark the changing of the seasons and remind us of important things that have happened to us on our journey—like leaving Egypt and getting the Torah at Mount Sinai."

Each week, they would now celebrate Shabbat, to remember the day of rest after the creation of the world. On Shabbat, they stopped moving, stopped working, and just took things slowly.

Once they arrived in the land of Canaan, they would celebrate Passover each spring, to remember the moment they left Egypt and became free people. They would taste matzah again, remembering the day they had to leave quickly and begin their journey.

From Passover until Shavuot, they would count forty-nine days to remember the exact time between when they left Egypt and when they received the Ten Commandments at Mount Sinai. This time of counting would be called the omer. With each day, they would get more and more excited, until finally it was time for Shavuot, a celebration to remember when Moses brought them the Torah from the top of Mount Sinai.

In the fall, they would sound the shofar for Rosh Hashanah, to begin a new year, and celebrate Sukkot in outdoor huts, sitting together and looking up at the stars in the sky.

Imagine Imagine yourself as an Israelite celebrating all of these holidays for the first time.

► Why do you think it was important for the Israelites to mark the big events that happened to them with holidays and festivals?

► Which holiday do you think was most important to them?

► What do you think it was like celebrating these holidays for the first time?

> Why do you think holidays are an important part of our calendar?

 Make Create a new holiday that celebrates a big moment in your own life!

► Think about a big moment in your life that you want to remember or celebrate. It could be the day you lost a tooth or moved to a new place. It could also be a day celebrating something you love (like superheroes or dinosaurs).

You'll Need
• large poster paper
• markers or crayons
• party decorations

► Create a name for your holiday. What will this day be called, and when in the year will it be celebrated?

► Design three actions or rituals that you could do on that holiday to celebrate the event or theme. (For example, if the holiday celebrates dinosaurs, you can make up a dance move as your favorite dinosaur, eat a snack without using your hands, and dress in colors that remind you of dinosaur skin and scales.)

► Now, it is time to celebrate. Create a poster in honor of your holiday. Draw pictures of the ways you celebrate the holiday on the poster. Make decorations that you can put up on the walls or on the table in honor of your holiday.

> What is your favorite holiday tradition?

► Celebrate by doing the rituals you invented, and teach them to someone else. Invite others to celebrate your holiday!

Play Play a game to explore the counting of the omer.

▶ Photocopy or trace the Omer Game Board Template (page 120). Color the spaces from 1 to 49 as you count up to 49 together, starting at the Sea of Reeds and culminating at Mount Sinai. (Each of these 49 spaces represents one of the 49 days counted between Passover and Shavuot.)

You'll Need

- Omer Game Board Template (page 120)
- crayons
- buttons (or game pieces)
- dice

▶ For older players, add challenges to a few of the squares along the board to either move a certain number of spaces ahead or back or skip a turn. You can reference different events from the Israelites' journey through the wilderness that we've explored so far. You can use these or make up your own:

- You've built the Tabernacle! Jump three steps forward.

- You complained about the food in the wilderness and said to Moses, "Take me back to Egypt!" Jump three steps back.

- You got sick with *tzara'at*! Skip a turn until you feel better.

▶ Find objects to be game board pieces (you can borrow them from another game or use different color buttons for each player).

▶ The first person takes a turn. Roll the dice, and move the corresponding number of spaces on the board.

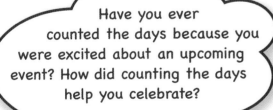
Have you ever counted the days because you were excited about an upcoming event? How did counting the days help you celebrate?

▶ The next person takes a turn.

▶ The first person to reach Mount Sinai and receive the Torah wins the game.

Omer Game Board Template

Color in the game board, and use it for the PLAY activity above.

CHAPTER 32

Give the Land a Break

Leviticus 25:1–26:2 • *Parashat B'har* • בְּהַר

**Learn about the tradition of *sh'mitah*, create a game
to play harvesting fruits and vegetables, and imagine
being a farmer who gives the land a rest!**

How do you take care of the earth around you?

The Israelites continued camping in the wilderness at the base of Mount Sinai, but they would soon start their journey toward the land of Canaan. Moses told them that once they finally arrive, they would need to think about how to take care of their new homeland. Just like people need a rest every week, the earth needs a break too.

An Israelite who dreamed of being a farmer perked up when he heard Moses share this instruction. "How can we give the land a time to rest?" the Israelite asked. "As a farmer, I will need the land to grow for me all the time. What would I do without it?"

Moses told them that every seven years, the Israelite and other farmers would need to give the land a rest. The seventh year would be called *sh'mitah*. In that year, the farmers would stop working the land and let it take a break. Any fruits or vegetables that grew on their own that year could be picked and taken by anyone. After the year was through, they could go back to farming as usual.

"I guess everyone needs a rest sometimes, even the earth," the hopeful farmer said as he looked down at the ground in the light of the sun.

Imagine Imagine yourself as an Israelite farmer taking a break and letting the land grow on its own.

▶ As a farmer, how do you think you would prepare for the *sh'mitah* year during the other six years?

▶ Why do you think you need to give the land a rest?

> Have you ever visited a farm? Do you have your own garden? What fruits and vegetables have you seen growing in the ground or from trees?

Make Make a card to say thank you to the land.

▶ Think about all of the things you use every day that come from the land.

▶ Write or draw your list, going through each part of your day. Think about the things you eat, wear, or use.

▶ Write a card to the land to say thank you. Make a collage on your card using recycled materials, like cut-up cardboard or plastic bottle pieces. You can draw a picture and use examples from your list in your card.

> **You'll Need**
> • paper
> • a pen or pencil
> • construction paper
> • markers or crayons
> • recycled materials

> How often do you need to take a rest? What do you do to rest after you've had a busy day?

▶ Take a walk around your neighborhood and say thank you to the land as you appreciate everything that it gives us.

▶ Think about ways you can take better care of the earth. Make a plan to be kinder to the world around you by recycling, composting, or using less water.

Explore Watch a seed sprout, and experiment with the best ways to help it grow.

▶ Moisten a napkin and place it in a jar.

▶ Moisten a cotton ball, place a bean inside of it, and push it up against the side of the jar (this way you'll be able to see the bean grow).

▶ Repeat these steps so that you have two open jars (no lids) with beans.

▶ Put one jar next to a sunny window and the other one in a dark cabinet.

> **You'll Need**
> • napkins
> • water
> • 2 jars
> • cotton balls
> • 2 dry beans (like lima beans)

▶ Check on your jars each day over the next few days. Add a little bit of water if the napkins or cotton balls get dry. What do you notice? How are the jars different? Which of the beans begins to sprout into a bean plant?

Play ## Pretend to be a farmer, and play a game to explore the sh'mitah year.

▶ Color the *Sh'mitah* Game Board Template (page 124).

▶ On the back of each fruit or vegetable square, grown-ups (or children who already write) can write a number between 1 and 7 using a pen or pencil (so that you can't see the number through the front).

▶ Cut out the squares. Mix them up, and lay them out on the floor, with the fruit or vegetable side up.

▶ Each person takes their own plastic bowl. The third bowl stands in the center away from the players.

▶ The players pretend to be farmers, and their spatulas or tongs are the tools.

> **You'll Need**
> - Sh'mitah Game Board Template (page 124)
> - markers
> - a pen or pencil
> - scissors
> - 3 small plastic bowls
> - 2 spatulas or tongs

▶ One at a time, each player picks one of the fruit or vegetable cards and turns it over. If the number on the back is between 1 and 6, the farmer can keep the card and put it in their bowl. If the number is 7, it represents fruits or vegetables grown in a *sh'mitah* year (seventh year), and it is ownerless. It goes in the cup in the center.

> What can you do to take care of the land and our planet?

▶ The first player to harvest ten fruits or vegetables of their own wins!

For Groups:

With multiple players, use several game boards to play this game in pairs or small groups.

Sh'mitah Game Board Template

Color in the fruits and vegetables, and cut them out. Follow the instructions in the PLAY activity on the previous page to play the game.

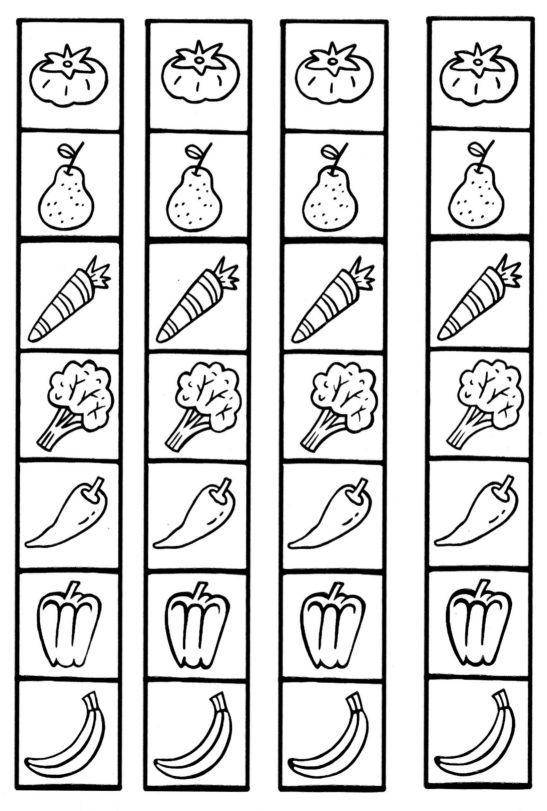

CHAPTER 33

A Mountain of Lessons

Leviticus 26:3–27:34 • *Parashat B'chukotai* • בְּחֻקֹּתַי

Review the lessons learned in the wilderness, climb down from Mount Sinai, and make your own Torah!

How do you remember things you've learned?

"I have shared my lessons with you," Moses told the Israelites. "That's everything that God wanted you to know for now." He finished teaching them lessons that God had taught him while he was up at the top of Mount Sinai, inside the cloud listening as hard as he could for forty days and forty nights. Moses felt tired, and his head hurt. He had been holding on to so many lessons and stories, trying to remember every detail, and now they were finally shared with all of the Israelites. He let out a sigh of relief.

The Israelites had learned about how to take care of each other in the wilderness, how to show gratitude for their community, and how to prepare for their new home when they arrived in the land of Canaan.

The people had learned a lot, and it was time to keep moving. "Where are we going now?" the Israelites asked.

"It's time to make our way toward Canaan—our future home," Moses said. "If we remember all of these lessons and stories and keep them safe, God will protect us in our adventures."

The Israelites packed up their tents and said goodbye to Mount Sinai as they traveled farther into the wilderness.

Imagine **Imagine yourself learning so many lessons from Moses while camped at the base of Mount Sinai.**

▶ Why do you think it was important for the Israelites to learn all of this after coming out of Egypt and before they made the rest of the journey to the land of Canaan?

▶ What do you think the Israelites did to remember everything they learned?

> What stories from the Torah have been your favorite so far? Why?

▶ Which lessons were most important to the Israelites?

 Make **Make your own Torah as a scrapbook of the lessons you've learned.**

▶ Review all of the stories and activities you've explored so far playing your way through the Bible. What moments stand out? What lessons were the most familiar? Which ones were the most surprising?

You'll Need
- paper
- markers
- scissors
- four popsicle sticks or paper towel rolls
- tape or glue

> Why do you think many people continue to read and learn about these stories today?

▶ On a piece of paper (landscape orientation), create a scrapbook of your memories from exploring these stories together. You can draw, write lessons learned, or print and glue any photos you took playing the activities together. Add a second or third piece of paper if you have more to include.

▶ Once you've created your scrapbook, attach the popsicle sticks or paper towel rolls vertically on the four corners of the paper using tape or glue.

▶ Roll up your piece of paper from both sides to create the scrolls of the Torah.

  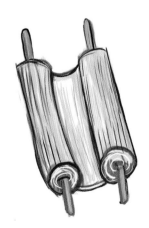

Play Create the peak of Mount Sinai, and act out the moment of climbing down the mountain after the Torah has been received and written.

▶ Create a pile of blankets and pillows. Construct the pillows like a mini-mountain.

▶ Use bedsheets to cover the pillows and make your mountain even bigger.

▶ Use flashlights or other colored lights to make the room feel more magical.

▶ Put your scrapbook Torah at the top.

You'll Need
- blankets
- pillows
- bedsheets
- flashlights
- your scrapbook Torah (from the MAKE activity above)

▶ Once you climb to the top of the mountain, find your scrapbook Torah and talk about all of the memories and lessons you learned together.

▶ Make the climb down the mountain holding the scrapbook Torah containing all of the lessons you learned over the last few months. It's time to continue the journey.

> What do you do to remember events or stories that happen in your life?

Completing Leviticus
A Celebration Ritual

You've just finished the book of Leviticus! You worked in the Tabernacle and learned what it means to be part of the Israelite community. Now you are ready to pack up your tent and begin the search for your new home. Well done! Let's mark this milestone together.

Unroll the Scroll

Imagine that you are the big scroll of the Torah. Stand really tall, with your arms at your sides. On the count of three, do *three* giant spins to pretend that you are unrolling the scroll past Genesis, Exodus, and Leviticus to the next section of the Torah.

One, two, three, spin!

Shout a Cheer

Say together in Hebrew, English or both:

"Chazak, chazak, v'nit'chazeik!"

"Be strong, be strong, and we'll be strong together!"

You can say these words together, or come up with your own cheer for Leviticus. (For example, "We learned! We grew! Let's move on now—me and you!")

Celebrate

Have a party in honor of everything you've created and explored. Wear your *kohein* uniform and make up a dance inspired by lighting the Menorah in the Tabernacle. Pretend like you are the land during the *sh'mitah* year and take a big rest. Plan how you want to mark the moment together, and celebrate your own way!

NUMBERS

OUR ADVENTURES THROUGH THE WILDERNESS

Follow the Israelites on their adventures across the desert and through the wilderness. They spend a long time wandering (forty whole years!), and there are many bumps along the way. As the Israelites dream of arriving in the land of Canaan, they complain a lot, test Moses's patience, and wonder if they'll ever reach their destination.

You'll find water springing out of a rock, encounter a talking donkey, and join scouts on a mission to check out the land of Canaan. Get ready to explore the wild wilderness!

CHAPTER 34

Everybody Counts

Numbers 1:1–4:20 • *Parashat B'midbar* • בְּמִדְבַּר

Get counting as you prepare to travel through the wilderness, and fly your flag high.

How do you make sure that everyone in your group stays together while on a trip?

It was finally time to leave Mount Sinai. The Israelites had learned so much while they camped there at the base of the mountain, but they were ready to head off into the wilderness to reach their permanent home.

"Are we all here?" Aaron asked as they began to pack up. "Has anyone wandered off? We need to check our numbers to make sure everyone stays together on our journey."

The Israelites would be moving through the desert with lots of people, animals, and luggage. Aaron realized they needed to count to make sure they knew how many people were traveling with the camp from place to place. "Gather around everyone! We need to count the people in the camp before we leave," Moses and Aaron told the Israelites.

Aaron led the big count off to make sure they knew their numbers before getting too far into the wilderness. "Okay, we've got that all written down," Aaron said as he counted the last Israelite. "Let's get going, and everyone stay together!"

Aaron looked behind him at the huge Israelite camp, raising their flags as they prepared to travel. Each of the twelve Israelite tribes had their own unique flag to represent their group, with colors and pictures that made it easier to find the way through the camp. If an Israelite ever got lost, the flags flew high in the air to guide them back to their tribe. "Flags up, and away we go!" Aaron said as they walked, the mountain getting smaller and smaller behind them in the distance.

 **Imagine** Imagine yourself preparing for the long journey into the wilderness after being camped at Mount Sinai.

▶ How do you think the Israelites felt, preparing to embark on their journey after spending a long time camping at Mount Sinai?

▶ Why do you think it was important for Aaron to count the Israelites before traveling through the wilderness?

▶ What type of designs do you imagine on the different Israelite flags?

> What are the things you like to count? What is the highest number you can count to?

 Make Design a flag to represent your family or classroom tribe.

▶ Think about the flags that the Israelites created for their tribes. Each one had an emblem and its own set of colors. For example, Judah's tribe had a lion on their flag, while Benjamin's had the image of a wolf.

You'll Need
- paper
- markers
- other craft supplies

> What famous flags do you know? What images do they have on them? Why do you think we have flags as symbols for countries or places?

▶ Think about how you would represent your family or your classroom on a flag. What is unique about you? What images, colors, or ideas might represent you?

▶ Once you have some ideas, design your flag on paper. Choose your favorite colors, and add any other pictures or symbols that represent your special characteristics on your flag.

Explore Count your stuffed animals, just like Aaron counted the Israelites.

▶ Think about the different types of stuffed animals you have. (If you prefer, you can use another object or toy type that you have a large amount of in your home or classroom, such as blocks or books.)

You'll Need
• paper
• markers
• various stuffed animals

▶ Create a census sheet to track the different categories of stuffed animals (for example: land animals, sea animals, dinosaurs, or TV characters).

▶ Write the category on the left, and draw a picture of the category in the middle. Then draw a line on the right where you'll write the corresponding number.

▶ For children who don't yet write, have a grown-up or older child create the census sheet, while the younger child gathers and categorizes the stuffed animals for the census.

▶ Lay out your stuffed animals. Put them into the category groups that you created.

▶ Count each group, and write the number down on your census sheet.

▶ Announce the results of the census to the crowd of stuffed animals.

For Groups:

With a classroom, you could invite the children to bring in some stuffed animals from home in advance of playing this activity.

Why do you think it's important to count groups of people before traveling from one place to another?

CHAPTER 35

Putting It Together

Numbers 4:21–7:89 • *Parashat Naso* • נָשֹׂא

**Build the Tabernacle piece by piece, take it apart,
and move it to the next campsite.**

How do you prepare to go on a big trip?

As the sun rose over the Israelite camp, excitement filled the air. The Israelites were on the move again, continuing their journey into the wilderness toward their new home. They took down their tents, packed their bags, prepared the camels, and most importantly, got ready to move the Tabernacle—their portable temple that God told them to build.

"We'll take the Tabernacle down, one piece at a time," the Levite tribe said. They had a very important job—the Levites were in charge of carrying all of the parts of the Tabernacle, setting it up piece by piece each time the Israelites stopped to rest at a campsite. They each carried different parts of the Tabernacle, working together to share the responsibility as they walked across the desert.

"We'll carry the Tabernacle tent covering!" said one group of Levites.

"We'll carry the poles!" said another group.

"And we'll take the bars, posts, and sockets!" said a third group.

When they arrived at the next campsite, the Levites would collect all of the parts and put them back together like a puzzle. At first it was difficult to remember how to put the Tabernacle together, but soon they had it memorized. They worked all day to put the Tabernacle in place, and as the moon appeared in the sky, they found their way back to their tents to rest.

"All right everyone, look for the Levite flag to find your way back to our part of the camp!" Aaron said as the Levites went back to their tents to rest after a long day on the move.

 **Imagine** Imagine yourself working together with the other Levites to take apart the Tabernacle, move it to a new camp, and put it back together again.

▶ Why do you think they needed to create specific jobs for taking down and building the Tabernacle in each place they camped?

▶ Which part of the Tabernacle would you want to carry?

▶ What do you think is the best part of belonging to a tribe?

> When you have gone on a journey or trip, where have you stayed overnight? How is it different from being in your own house?

 Explore Construct your tabletop tent, take it down, transport it, and reassemble it in a new location.

▶ Lay the materials in front of you: cups, napkins, forks, aluminum foil, and string. Challenge yourself to use these materials to create a tabletop tent, imagining the tent in the Tabernacle.

▶ Try to use all of the materials as part of your construction. Can you create a tent that stands on its own?

You'll Need
• 4 paper or plastic cups
• paper napkins
• 4 plastic forks
• aluminum foil
• string

▶ Once you have a structure you like, disassemble it so that the materials are separated again.

▶ Decide who will be in charge of each of the materials (for example, one person will manage the cups, while another person will hold the aluminum foil).

▶ Each person can pick up their assigned material and together transport the materials to a different location in the room. Imagine that you are like the Levite tribe, with each person assigned to transport a different material from the Tabernacle.

> What routines do you do in a specific order (like getting ready for bed)? Do you ever change the routine?

▶ Find a new tabletop location in a different spot, and put the materials down.

▶ Now, reassemble your tabletop tent in the same order that you used to construct it originally.

Play Create a sequence of movements, and put it together like the pieces of the Tabernacle.

> **You'll Need**
> • paper
> • a pen

▶ Think about how the Levites had to put together the pieces of the Tabernacle in a particular order. Each person had to put their piece in place.

▶ Use your body and imaginations to create a sequence of movements that you can build together.

▶ Each person creates a shape or movement using their body (with two players, each person can create two moves). You can use the structure of the Tabernacle as inspiration for your movements or make up any silly shape with your body. For example, you can stretch your hands up high to be a pole or stretch your fingers down to the floor in front of you to be a tent.

▶ Draw a small picture of each movement in order on a piece of paper to help you remember them.

▶ Learn and practice each of the movements.

▶ Put them all together and connect them to become one dance series. Everyone can perform the dance together at the same time.

▶ Try putting on music and performing your dance series to the beat!

> Have you ever put together a puzzle or built something big with a group? How did you work together?

CHAPTER 36

Are We There Yet?!

Numbers 8:1–12:16 • *Parashat B'ha'alot'cha* • בְּהַעֲלֹתְךָ

Follow the cloud as you navigate your way through the desert, and design your dream meal for traveling through the wilderness.

Have you ever complained about a long trip you had to take?

"The cloud is on the move . . . let's go everyone!" Moses called out from his tent. The Israelites journeyed through the wilderness in the hot sun, day after day. At each new campsite, they couldn't predict when it was time to go and when it was time to stop. They followed the movement of a special cloud that God used to direct them. When the cloud lifted into the air, it was time to journey onward. When the cloud came down to rest over the camp, it was time to stop. Go. Stop. Go. Stop. Go. Stop!

As they walked and walked, the Israelites complained to Moses *a lot* about the journey. "Moses, we're so tired! Moses, we're so thirsty! Are we there yet?!" they whined.

They were also tired of eating manna, the special food that God provided to them on the journey. Sure, it tasted like sweet honey wafers . . . but they wanted meat! They dreamed about all the new meals they could make when they finally arrived in the land of Canaan. But . . . for now, they had to follow the cloud.

Even Miriam and Aaron were feeling grumpy. "Why does Moses get to be the leader all the time? It isn't fair—there's nothing that special about him anyway," Miriam grumbled angrily to Aaron as they walked.

God heard Miriam say this. "It isn't nice to talk about your brother that way," God said. "You need to take a break from the camp to think about making a better choice next time."

Miriam moved her tent outside of the camp for seven days. She thought about what she had said behind her brother's back. "No matter how angry I get, it isn't nice to say mean things about my brother," Miriam thought as she returned to camp.

Miriam gave her brothers a big hug, and the Israelites kept moving toward the next campsite.

Imagine **Imagine yourself following the cloud through the desert and complaining along the way.**

▶ Do you think you would get tired of eating the same food every day if you were an Israelite traveling through the desert? What foods would you miss if you only had manna to eat?

▶ How would you feel if you were Moses, listening to all of the Israelites complaining every day along the journey?

▶ How do you think Moses felt after Miriam said mean things about him?

> Have you ever complained about a trip or journey while you were on your way? Why?

Make **Design your dream meal for traveling through the wilderness as you wish for anything but manna to eat.**

▶ Imagine that you are an Israelite who only had manna to eat every day in the wilderness. Think of a meal that you wish you had instead. Draw the meal of your dreams, using construction paper and markers.

You'll Need
• construction paper
• markers
• scissors
• a plate

▶ Cut each of the pieces out, and put your dream meal on the plate.

▶ How would you feel getting to eat this meal? Act out that feeling as you pretend to eat.

> Which foods do you get tired of eating? Are there foods that you never get tired of eating?

Play Use the cloud to guide the Israelites through the wilderness.

▶ Cut out a piece of white paper in the shape of a cloud. Attach it to a blue piece of construction paper for the sky.

▶ Practice lifting the cloud above your head in the air and lowering it down to the ground.

▶ Play a game to imagine how the cloud guided the Israelites. Decide who will be the Cloud, and who will be the Israelites.

▶ When the person holding the cloud holds the sign down low, the Israelite stops. When they hold the sign high above their head, the Israelite starts to walk forward.

You'll Need
• white paper
• blue construction paper
• markers
• scissors
• tape

Have you ever said something mean about a friend or a sibling? How did it make them feel? What choice could you have made instead? Why is it important to be careful with the words we use?

▶ You can play this game around the room as a Follow-the-Leader game, with the Cloud deciding when to rest and when to travel. It can also be played similarly to the game Red Light, Green Light, with the Israelite trying to reach the destination of the land of Canaan.

CHAPTER 37

The Adventures of the Scouts

Numbers 13:1–15:41 • *Parashat Sh'lach L'cha* • שְׁלַח-לְךָ

Join the scouts to explore the land of Canaan, discover massive grapes and giant people on your trip, and report back to the Israelite camp.

Have you ever explored a place you'd never been to before?

"We're getting close to Canaan!" an Israelite named Caleb said to his friend Joshua. "I think I can see it in the distance!"

After traveling through the wilderness for a long time, the cloud led the Israelites to a campsite near the land of Canaan. Moses sent twelve scouts, one person from each of the tribes, into the land to scope out the scene and report back. Caleb and Joshua were chosen to be part of the mission. "I wonder what we'll find there!" Joshua said to Caleb as they waved goodbye to the campsite to cross into Canaan.

When they got back, the Israelites gathered around, anxious to hear about their trip. "What did you find there? Is it as wonderful as we imagine?" the people asked.

The scouts shared stories of seeing giant fruit in a lush and beautiful land. "Listen to this. . . . The grapes are so big they're the size of your head!" Caleb told them.

"The land really does flow with milk and honey. It's amazing!" Joshua chimed in.

But the rest of the scouts warned that the people living in the land were so big and scary they made the scouts feel small. "They were like giants, and they made us feel as tiny as grasshoppers!" some of the scouts said.

They warned that the people in the land didn't want the Israelites there. "We should have stayed in Egypt!" the people cried to Moses, scared of what they would find in Canaan.

Caleb and Joshua tried to tell the Israelites that it would be okay and that God would protect them if they went into Canaan according to plan. But the people didn't listen. God decided the Israelites weren't ready to enter the land. They would need to continue to travel through the desert until it was the right time to enter Canaan.

 **Imagine** **Imagine yourself scoping out the land and reporting back to the Israelites.**

▶ Why do you think Moses decided to send scouts into the land first, rather than just leading all of the people right into the land?

▶ How do you think the scouts felt as they explored the land together for the first time?

▶ Why do you think the Israelites said they wanted to go back to Egypt, even though their lives there were so hard?

> Think of a time you explored a new place. What did you bring with you? How did you feel? What did you find there?

 Explore **Become a scout and see what you find in your own neighborhood.**

▶ Roll a piece of construction paper from two sides to create binoculars. Tape the cylinders in place.

▶ Look out a window or take a walk outside, looking through your binoculars. What do you see? Do you notice anything interesting?

▶ Write or draw a list of five things you spied out of the window or on your walk, and share your findings with someone else. Did you notice anything new that you hadn't noticed before?

▶ Tell a story about what you saw, and describe everything in detail.

> **You'll Need**
> • construction paper
> • tape

> **Tip:**
> Save your binoculars to use again in chapter 54.

 **Make** **Imagine you are one of the scouts, and create the scene of what you saw on your adventure.**

▶ Draw a picture of what the scouts said they saw when they entered the land. Ideas include really big grapes, people who made the scouts feel as tiny as grasshoppers, and a land flowing with milk and honey.

▶ Use your toys to bring your drawing to life. Create the scene of the scouts discovering the land in miniature. What can you use for the giant fruit? How can you use plastic building blocks and other materials to create the land of Canaan?

▶ Use your imagination, your craft supplies, and your toys to re-create the scene from your picture.

> **You'll Need**
> • paper
> • markers
> • plastic building blocks
> • small toy figures

Play Bring your scout scene to life by acting out what the scouts reported back to the Israelites.

▶ Bring your miniature scene to life by acting out the version of the story that Caleb and Joshua shared. Move your miniature figures through the landscape you created. Use your voices to say what Caleb and Joshua might have been thinking as they explored the land for the first time.

> **You'll Need**
> • the miniature scene you built (from the MAKE activity)

• You could say: "Wow! Look at this incredible place. There are so many incredible fruits and vegetables growing here!"

▶ Act out the version that the rest of the scouts shared. Use your body and your voice to pretend to be the giant people the other scouts imagined they saw.

> *What are the different ways that you can share details of your journey with someone who didn't come with you?*

▶ Use a big giant voice, and stomp around the toys, pretending that they are the scouts as you scare them away from the land.

For Groups:

You could have one group act out the Caleb and Joshua version, while the other group acts out what the rest of the scouts reported. Each group can share while the other group watches as an audience.

Korach Makes Some Trouble

Numbers 16:1–18:32 • *Parashat Korach* • קֹרַח

Act out the moment that Korach enters the Tabernacle without permission, and make flowers bloom from Aaron's staff.

Have you ever been angry with a rule made by someone in charge?

"Why are Moses and Aaron always in charge? Aaron and his sons are the only ones who get to do the most important jobs in the Tabernacle. It's just not fair," an Israelite named Korach grumbled.

As the Israelites wandered through the wilderness, Korach felt fed up. Instead of talking to Moses and Aaron, he complained about them to other Israelites, who started to feel angry too. Korach and his followers marched to the front of the Tabernacle to yell at Moses and Aaron.

"It isn't fair that you get to be in charge! Why do you think you are more important than the rest of us?" they screamed.

When Moses heard them yelling at him and Aaron, he fell to the ground. "We didn't make these rules. God gave us these jobs!" Moses said. "Everyone in the camp has an important part to play, including you!"

But Korach and his followers were too angry to listen.

"I'll show you once and for all who I want to work inside of the Tabernacle," God said. God told Moses that each of the tribes should bring a staff to the tent with their name written on it. "Line them all up in a row. The staff of the chosen tribe will sprout."

The Israelites did just that. Suddenly, something incredible happened. "Look at Aaron's staff!" the Israelites whispered, as they saw beautiful flowers bloom from the top. It was a clear sign that he and his family were supposed to be in charge of working in the Tabernacle. "We all play an important role in our community," Aaron said. "We have to trust each other instead of fighting and complaining all the time." The Israelites understood that they had to behave like a team if they were going to make it through the wilderness together.

Imagine Imagine yourself sneaking around and making a plot to betray Moses.

▶ Why do you think Korach was so upset with Moses and Aaron?

▶ How would you feel if only a few people were chosen to do an important job?

▶ Can you imagine a different choice that Korach could have made to explain why he was upset, instead of getting everyone to yell at Moses and Aaron? What might you have done differently?

> How have you been unhappy with the rules and decisions made by someone in charge?

 Make Create the flowers that bloomed from Aaron's staff.

▶ Stack a few pieces of tissue paper or paper towels on top of one another.

▶ Use the markers to gently color and decorate the tissue paper or paper towel as flowers.

▶ Fold the tissue paper into a long horizontal strip.

▶ Wrap the top of the pipe cleaner around the middle of the tissue paper. The pipe cleaner will be the stem of the flowers.

▶ Fluff the tissue paper at the sides, and bring the two sides to the middle at the top to make the shape of a flower.

> **You'll Need**
> • tissue paper or paper towel
> • markers
> • pipe cleaner
> • cardboard tube

▶ Hide your flower inside the cardboard tube, imagining the tube is Aaron's staff.

▶ Use your staff in the next activity.

> What are some positive ways to handle your feelings when you are frustrated?

Play **Act out the moment when flowers bloom from Aaron's staff to show that he is supposed to be in charge of the Tabernacle.**

▶ Decide who will play Aaron and who will play Korach.

▶ Create the entrance of the Tabernacle using a bedsheet and chairs.

▶ Korach says, "It isn't fair that you get to be in charge! Why do you think you are more important than the rest of us?" Korach is really upset. How can you show how Korach is feeling using your face and your body movement?

▶ Aaron brings his staff to the entrance of the tent.

> **You'll Need**
> • a bedsheet
> • chairs
> • the staff and flower (from the MAKE activity)

▶ On the count of three, slowly raise the flower up through the tube to reveal it on the top, just like Aaron's staff suddenly sprouted flowers in the story.

> Do you think it is hard being in charge and making the rules? Why or why not?

▶ Aaron says, "Look! It's a sign that I'm supposed to work in the Tabernacle. Everyone has an important job, and we need to work as a team!"

▶ Now switch roles, so that everyone has a chance to play Aaron and Korach.

For Groups:

With multiple players, you can have half of the group play Korach and half of the group play Aaron. You can also start with two people acting out the scene, while the rest of the group watches as the audience. Take turns playing each of the roles.

CHAPTER 39

Talk to the Rock

Numbers 19:1–22:1 • *Parashat Chukat* • חֻקַּת

Complain about being thirsty, and make water spring from a rock.

How do you ask for something you need?

"We're so thirsty, Moses! What are we going to do?" complained the Israelites, standing in the hot sun. There, in the middle of the dry desert, the people couldn't find any water to drink.

Moses didn't know what to do, so he asked God. "Take your staff, and bring the whole community together by the rock in the center of camp," God told him. "Go speak to the rock, and tell it to give you water. Refreshing cold water will spring out for everyone to drink."

Moses tried to follow the instructions, but the people complained even more. "Moses, you'll never find us water to drink!" they shouted. "We should have stayed in Egypt! At least there we had water to drink!"

Moses got frustrated with all of their complaining. Instead of speaking to the rock as God had instructed, Moses raised his staff in the air and hit the rock! To everyone's surprise, water sprung from it, and the people finally had water to drink . . . but God was upset with Moses for not following the directions.

"Moses, you should have trusted me. I told you to talk to the rock, but you didn't believe that it would work," God said.

Moses realized that he had made a mistake. Even leaders sometimes don't know what to do. Next time, Moses would try to take a deep breath and remember to stay calm before making a decision.

Imagine Imagine yourself getting distracted by the Israelites complaining and hitting the rock instead of talking to it.

▶ How would you feel if the Israelites kept complaining and complaining no matter what you did?

▶ What do you think Moses should have done when the people kept complaining?

> Have you ever been really frustrated? What did you do to calm down?

 Explore Experiment with water and sponges as you imagine water springing from the rock.

▶ Lay a towel over the table so that you don't make too much of a mess.

▶ Fill the measuring cups with water.

▶ Start with the smallest cup first. Put the sponge in the bowl, and slowly pour the water onto the sponge. See if you can get the sponge to absorb the water.

▶ Now, hold up the sponge and say to it, "Rock, give us water!" Squeeze the sponge to make the water come out into the bowl.

> **You'll Need**
> • a towel
> • water
> • measuring cups of various sizes
> • a sponge
> • a large bowl

▶ Continue this experiment as you increase the amount of water that the sponge holds, using the larger measuring cups. See how much water you can get the sponge to absorb and release!

▶ You can also try this experiment with a variety of rocks, to see if any rocks can absorb water. Porous rocks like sandstone and pumice will absorb more water than granite and shale. What kind of rock do you think sprung water in the story?

> What do you do when you know the instructions you are supposed to follow but other people are telling you to do something else?

Play Act out the moment when the water comes bursting from the rock.

▶ Decide who will be Moses and who will be the rock.

▶ The rock can curl up under a blanket and hold the spray bottle.

▶ Act out the scene as God instructed: Moses can ask the rock to offer water to the people. When he asks, the rock can spray the water as a mist above.

> **You'll Need**
> • blanket
> • misting spray bottle filled with water
> • stick

> What are the best ways to ask for something that you need?

▶ Act out the scene as it happened: Moses can hold up a stick and pretend to hit the rock, and the rock can spray water as a mist above.

▶ Now, switch roles so that everyone can play Moses and the rock.

For Groups:

With multiple players, you can have half of the group play Moses and half of the group play the rock. Spread out in pairs and act out the scene at the same time. You can also have the rest of the group act out the role of the complaining Israelites in the scene.

CHAPTER 40

Balaam and the Talking Donkey

Numbers 22:2–25:9 • *Parashat Balak* • בָּלָק

Follow Balaam as he tries to curse the Israelites, meet a talking donkey, and share some unexpected blessings.

Why is it important to be careful with the words we use and the things we say to each other?

As the Israelites traveled through the wilderness, they passed by other communities of people.

"I don't want those Israelites wandering through our land," King Balak said, looking out from his tent at the top of a tall mountain in the wilderness.

King Balak and his people, the Moabites, didn't trust the Israelites. Balak decided to try to stop them from passing through their kingdom. He said, "I will send my advisor Balaam to put a curse on the Israelites. They will never reach the land."

Balaam got on his donkey and set off to do as Balak had ordered. On his way to curse the Israelites, Balaam's donkey stopped in her tracks and refused to keep moving. "Keep going, donkey!" Balaam yelled. "Why did you stop?!"

But the donkey was frozen in place. Suddenly, the donkey used her voice and talked back to him. "I've been carrying you all this way, but I won't go any farther," she yelled. "Look up and you'll see why."

Balaam looked up and saw an angel sent from God standing in front of the donkey. He felt afraid. "I'm sorry I didn't see you before. If you want me to turn back, I will!" Balaam said nervously to the angel.

But the angel said, "No! Keep going, but you'll only say what I tell you to say once you get there."

Balaam slowly continued down the path, not sure what would happen. He arrived at the top of a hill, overlooking all of the Israelite camp. When Balaam opened his mouth to shout his curse, blessings came out instead. He moved to a different spot, trying again. He opened his mouth to shout an even louder, meaner curse . . . and an even more beautiful blessing came out!

Full of Balaam's blessings, the Israelites set up their campsite in Balak's kingdom and rested there before continuing their journey.

Imagine Imagine yourself trying (and failing) to curse the Israelites.

▶ How do you think the Israelites felt traveling through the kingdoms of other people in the wilderness?

▶ How would you react if you were Balaam and your donkey started to talk?

▶ What do you think Balaam thought when blessings came out of his mouth instead of the curses he was thinking?

> If you had the power to make an animal talk to you, which animal would you choose and why?

 Make Create Balaam and Donkey puppets, and bring their journey to life.

▶ Photocopy or trace and color the Balaam and Donkey Puppet Template (page 153).

▶ Cut them out, and attach them to chopsticks or straws to make them into puppets.

▶ Find a good table or chair to be a puppet stage. Sit behind the table or chair so that you can create the puppet performance in front of you for your audience.

▶ Create the scenery where the story takes place. You can arrange fabric pieces (scarves or dish towels) or aluminum foil on the table or chair to make a desert landscape for the puppets to walk across. Try to create the shape of a hill and a valley. (Alternatively, you can play this activity outside in a sandbox, and use the sand to create your puppet landscape.)

▶ Add a lamp shining from above the scene to be the hot sun. What else can you use to build the scenery of the story on your puppet stage?

You'll Need
- Balaam and Donkey Puppet Template (page 153)
- crayons or markers
- scissors
- chopsticks or straws
- tape
- aluminum foil or various fabric pieces (scarves or dish towels)
- a lamp or flashlight

Play Bring the story of Balaam and the donkey to life as a puppet show.

▶ Decide who will be Balaam and who will be Donkey.

▶ Experiment with how the two characters move and what they sound like. Use your voice and your hand movements to bring the characters to life.

> **You'll Need**
> • Balaam and Donkey puppets (from the MAKE activity above)

▶ Start the scene with Donkey leading the way and Balaam following.

▶ Donkey stops on the journey. Balaam says to Donkey, "Why did you stop? Keep moving!"

▶ Donkey turns around and says, "I've been carrying you all this way, but I won't go any farther!"

▶ How do you think Balaam reacts when he realizes that his donkey can talk? Act out your reaction.

▶ After acting out this scene, switch roles.

Play Act out the moment when Balaam's curses turn into blessings.

▶ Think of something really nice you can say to each other. It can be a blessing or just a compliment. (For example: "I hope you have a wonderful life!" or "You are amazing just the way you are!")

▶ Cross your arms or point your finger in front of you, like you are about to say something really mean. What kind of expression can you make on your face? How would you stand?

> Have you ever thought about saying something mean but then stopped yourself from saying it? Why did you make a different choice?

▶ On the count of three, say your blessing or compliment to the other person, but use a really angry and mean voice when you say it. Make the sound of your voice like a curse but the words that you say a blessing!

Balaam and Donkey Puppet Template

Cut out each of the shapes below and attach them to chopsticks or straws using tape. Use them as puppets in the MAKE and PLAY activities above.

CHAPTER 41

The Sisters Who Spoke Up

Numbers 25:10–30:1 • *Parashat Pinchas* • פִּינְחָס

Meet the daughters of Zelophehad, speak up for your rights, and explore the ways we can advocate for fairness in our rules.

Have you ever thought it was unfair when someone told you that you couldn't do something?

"Where will we build our homes in Canaan?" the Israelites wondered.

In the wilderness, the people started to make plans for where they would live in the land of Canaan. According to the rules, each man would be given a portion of land where he could build a home for his family. "I can't wait to build a beautiful place to live when we get there," Hoglah said.

Even though her father Zelophehad was no longer living, Hoglah and her four sisters—Noa, Milcah, Mahlah, and Tirzah—planned to make a home on their own together. Noa said, "We'll remember our father every day as we build a house on the land that would have been his."

But they soon learned that couldn't happen. According to the rules, their father's land could be passed down only to sons, not daughters. "That's not fair!" said Mahlah.

She and her four sisters marched straight to the Tabernacle to meet with Moses. They stood side by side, in front of the tent. "It's not right that we can't get this land just because we are girls!" Milcah said to him. "Why can't we have it as our own?"

Moses took their question to God. "What do I do? How should I solve their case?" he asked.

"The sisters are right," God said. "Make a change to the law, and give the sisters their fair share of the land."

The sisters were proud—not just because they would be able to build their house, but they changed the law to be fairer for those who came after them.

 **Imagine yourself as one of the daughters of Zelophehad coming to make their case.**

▶ Why do you think the daughters of Zelophehad wanted to be in charge of their father's land?

▶ How do you think the daughters of Zelophehad felt when they found out they couldn't be in charge of their father's land just because they were girls?

▶ Why do you think the law was changed?

> Think about a time when you felt a rule was unfair. How did you share your feelings about it? How did the rule change?

 Design the daughters of Zelophehad, and bring them to life as paper dolls.

▶ Copy the Daughters of Zelophehad Paper Dolls Template. (page 157)

▶ Cut out the rectangle along the solid line border.

▶ Fold the strip of paper in fifths like an accordion along the vertical lines. The image of the character should be at the front with the folded sections behind.

▶ Cut along the dotted line around the shape of the figure, keeping the folds in place.

▶ Unfold the paper to reveal the shape of the five connected daughters of Zelophehad.

▶ Decorate the daughters of Zelophehad using markers and crayons.

▶ You can fold another piece of paper in half, and decorate it to be the Tent of Meeting, outside of which the daughters met with Moses.

You'll Need
- Daughters of Zelophehad Paper Dolls Template (page 157)
- paper
- markers
- scissors

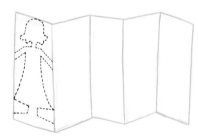

Play Bring the story of the daughters of Zelophehad to life.

▶ Act out the moment when the daughters come to Moses asking to change the law.

▶ One person can play Moses while the other person puppeteers the daughters.

> **You'll Need**
> • daughters of Zelophehad paper dolls (from the MAKE activity)

> Have you ever admitted that you were wrong about a rule you made? What change did you make to your rule, and how were things different afterward?

▶ The daughters can say, "It's not right that we can't get this land just because we are girls!"

▶ Moses can say, "Hmm. I'm not sure. I will talk this over with God." Moses can leave the room and then come back and say, "You are right. God said we should change the law."

▶ Now switch roles so that everyone has a chance to make their case.

For Groups:

With multiple players, you can have half of the group play the daughters and half of the group play Moses. Alternatively, you can act out this scene with people instead of puppets, with five people getting to take on the role of one of the daughters. Take turns playing each of the roles.

Daughters of Zelophehad Paper Dolls Template

Use this template to create the daughters of Zelophehad as paper dolls for the MAKE activity.

CHAPTER 42

A Cozy Spot for the Cattle

Numbers 30:2–32:42 • Parashat Matot • מַטּוֹת

Find the perfect spot for you and your cattle to settle, and help the rest of your neighbors find their own spot to build a home too.

What is the environment like where you live?

While the Israelites camped in the wilderness, they thought about what life would be like once they arrived in the land of Canaan. "Where will we all live once we get there?" they thought to themselves each night, dreaming of their new home.

One night while they camped, the Israelites had a big meeting to plan where each tribe would live once they settled in Canaan. "Maybe we should be near the water," thought one tribe.

"Maybe we should be where there are lots of trees for shade from the sun," thought another.

Then the tribes of Reuben and Gad asked a question. "Moses, as you know, we have lots of cows," they said, pointing to the very large herd happily roaming around the pasture. "Can we just live on the east side of the river, near where we are now? This part of the land has lots of grass, and it will be the perfect place for our cows to graze."

Moses started to get angry about their request. "What about the rest of the tribes? How will they be able to set up the land across the river without your help?" he asked them. "Are you just going to stay here?"

The tribes of Reuben and Gad thought about this. "How about we come with you and help everyone unpack on that side. The cows will help too!" they said. "Once all of the other tribes are settled, we can come back to set up the perfect pasture on this side."

Everyone agreed that it was a great plan . . . especially the cows.

Imagine **Imagine yourself deciding which part of Canaan would be right for your tribe as you prepare to make a permanent home.**

▶ How do you think the Israelites decided how to divide up the land?

▶ What do you think they would do if two different tribes wanted the same part of the land?

▶ How would you decide what kind of land you wanted to build your house on in Canaan? What would be important to you?

> What do you like about the place where you live? What makes it different from other places you've visited?

Explore Plant grass seeds to understand what you need for creating a good pasture for your cows.

▶ Go on a walk around your neighborhood to find examples of healthy grass.

▶ Observe the grass with your senses. Look at it from different angles, smell it, and touch it gently. What do you notice? What do you think the grass needs to stay healthy?

▶ Back inside, plant some grass of your own. Grass is an important part of what cows eat in a healthy pasture.

▶ Fill a plastic cup more than halfway up with potting soil.

▶ Put about a dozen grass seeds inside, and gently cover them with soil.

▶ Moisten the soil by spraying it with water, using the spray bottle.

▶ Put plastic wrap over the cup to keep in the moisture. (When you start to notice the grass sprouting, take the plastic off the cup.)

▶ Place your cup in a sunny spot, and make sure the soil stays moist.

▶ Each day for a week, observe your cup. What do you notice? How many days does it take to see grass sprouting from the soil?

▶ What does grass need to grow? What do you think the tribes of Reuben and Gad noticed about the land on the east side of the river that made it good for their cows?

You'll Need
• a plastic cup
• potting soil
• grass seeds
• a spray bottle
• plastic wrap

Play   Create a pasture for your cows, and pretend to care for them.

▶ Arrange four chairs as the four corners of a big square.

▶ Tie or tape string between each of the chairs to create a big square pen. Imagine this as the pasture next to your plot of land in your new home in Canaan.

▶ Take a few stuffed animals, and imagine they are the cows in your pasture. Arrange them inside the pen.

▶ How can you care for your cows? What do they need? Pretend that there is food and water inside the plastic bowls, and go from cow to cow to feed them.

▶ Pretend to milk the cows, and collect the milk in the bowls. Pet the cows, and ask how they are doing. You can also make the sound of your cows (*"Moooooo!"*).

> **You'll Need**
> • four chairs
> • string
> • tape
> • stuffed animals
> • plastic bowls

> Have you ever taken care of animals? What did they need you to do for them? How did this responsibility make you feel?

160

CHAPTER 43

Remembering the Way

Numbers 33:1–36:13 • *Parashat Masei* • מַסְעֵי

Imagine the journey from campsite to campsite, and make your
way across the wilderness toward the land of Canaan.

What do you do to remember the places you've been?

"We're almost there! We're ready to enter the land this time!" the Israelites said as they looked at the Jordan River from their campsite. They could see the land of Canaan just on the other side of the banks. They were so close to the land of Canaan after wandering through the wilderness for a long time.

"We need to remember all of the places we've been so you don't forget about the long journey we took to get here," Moses said. "I'm going to make a list so that you always know where you've been once you are settled in your new home."

Moses wrote down all of the places that the Israelites had camped, from the time they left Egypt all the way to their campsite near the Jordan River.

Their journey began with a walk across the hot sand out of Egypt. They crossed the Sea of Reeds on their way into the wilderness.

"We could never forget that miracle. The water split into two so that we could cross!" one of the Israelites remembered.

After days and days of traveling, they came to a place called Elim. It was filled with water springs and many palm trees. "That was a beautiful place to rest after all that walking!" Moses remembered.

They journeyed from Elim all the way to Mount Sinai, where they camped to receive the Ten Commandments.

From Sinai, they journeyed for a long time—camping and moving and camping and moving again.

"Look at all the places we've been!" they said, amazed by the path they took to get to their campsite.

"Very soon, this journey will be behind you, and you'll be building your new home in the land of Canaan," Moses said. "But our adventures through the wilderness made you ready to become the people you are today."

Imagine **Imagine yourself traveling through the wilderness with Moses across many different campsites and adventures.**

▶ Why do you think Moses wanted to write down all of the different stops along the journey that they took through the wilderness?

▶ How do you think the people felt looking back at their journey, from leaving Egypt to arriving at the Jordan River?

> What place do you remember visiting with your family on a trip? What sights, sounds, smells, and activities do you remember from that place?

 Make **Design the Israelites' journey from campsite to campsite.**

▶ Create four signs to represent four of the Israelite campsites in the wilderness. On the first piece of paper, write the number "1," and draw a picture of a mound of sand.

▶ On the second, write the number "2," and draw a picture of water springs and palm trees.

▶ On the third, write the number "3," and draw a picture of a mountain.

▶ On the last, write the number "4," and draw a tent with stars and moon above.

▶ Use these signs in the next PLAY activity.

You'll Need
- paper
- markers

Play Navigate the Israelites' journey through various places in the wilderness.

> Go outside to a backyard, park, or playground (you can adapt to play indoors). Find four trees or posts on which to tape these four signs. (If you are playing this activity indoors, put the signs in four different rooms or the corners of one room).

> Start at sign number 1. Imagine you are packing up to go from one campsite to the next.

> Look at the picture on the sign, and imagine making the journey from sign 1 to 2, walking like you are traveling across hot sand.

> From 2 to 3, move like you are walking under beautiful palm trees and feel the water from the springs.

> From 3 to 4, pretend to climb up and down a steep mountain.

> When you get to campsite 4, get underneath the bedsheet and pretend it is a tent. Take a rest from your big journey.

You'll Need
- campsite signs (from the MAKE activity above)
- masking tape
- a bedsheet

What do you do to remember the adventures you take with your family or friends? Do you take pictures, collect souvenirs, or tell stories to your friends when you come home?

Completing Numbers
A Celebration Ritual

You've just finished the book of Numbers! You wandered through the desert, snuck a peek at your future home in Canaan, and followed the cloud on many adventures. You are almost at the end of your journey. Phew! Nicely done. Let's mark this milestone together.

Unroll the Scroll

Imagine that you are the big scroll of the Torah. Stand really tall, with your arms at your sides. On the count of three, do *four* giant spins to pretend that you are unrolling the scroll past Genesis, Exodus, Leviticus, and Numbers to the last section of the Torah. One, two, three, spin!

Shout a Cheer

Say together in Hebrew, English, or both:

"Chazak, chazak, v'nit'chazeik!"

"Be strong, be strong, and we'll be strong together!"

You can say these words together, or come up with your own cheer for Numbers. (For example, "Step by step, we walked and roamed; we're almost there, to our new home!")

Celebrate

Have a party to celebrate all of the adventures you've had in the wilderness. Dance like you're moving across hot sand. Sneak around the room like you are scouting out the land of Canaan. Splash some water in the sink or tub to cool off from the heat. Plan how you want to mark the moment together, and celebrate your own way!

DEUTERONOMY

FINDING OUR PLACE TO CALL HOME

Listen to Moses as he prepares the Israelites to finally cross over into the land of Canaan. He reminds them of the adventures they've been on and the lessons they've learned along the way. He appoints a new leader, Joshua, to lead the Israelites into the next chapter of their story. And he gets a look at the land of Canaan from the top of a tall mountain, seeing the beautiful destination after so many years of wandering.

You'll sing a song with Moses, make final preparations for building a community in Canaan, and get ready to take your first steps across the river and into your new home.

CHAPTER 44

Words from the Wilderness

Deuteronomy 1:1–3:22 • *Parashat D'varim* • דְּבָרִים

Recount the journey through the wilderness in an obstacle course, and deliver a speech to the Israelite people.

How do you get ready for a big change?

"Gather around, everyone. I want to share some words before our journey is over," Moses said to the people. Moses couldn't believe that it was almost time to finish this journey, after so many adventures in the wilderness.

The Israelites were finally close to the land of Canaan, the place they would soon call home. They camped at the edge of the Jordan River, the border that stood between them and Canaan. After many, many years of camping, their journey was almost complete.

Before it was time to enter the land, Moses wanted to make sure that the Israelites remembered everything they had learned along the way, from leaving Egypt to arriving at the Jordan River. They had been in the desert for forty years—moving the Tabernacle, learning how to work together, and following the lessons they learned at Mount Sinai such a long time before.

Moses slowly climbed up a hill and stood at the very top. He took a deep breath and looked out at his people. Finally, he started to deliver a big speech. "Before you go forward into the land, you have to look back at where you've been," Moses told the people.

He began to retell the story of their adventures, review lessons they'd learned, and remind them of everything they needed to know before building their new home in Canaan. "I still have so much to share with you, and I need to make sure you understand all of it before you enter Canaan," he said. The people sat around the hill looking up, quietly listening to every word.

 **Imagine yourself listening as Moses gives a big speech before you make your way into Canaan.**

▶ How do you think you would feel listening to Moses as he gave his speech to the people, reminding you of your journey?

▶ What do you think are the most important events that happened to the Israelites along the way from Egypt to Canaan?

▶ How do you think the people felt remembering all of the places they'd been and the things they'd learned along the way?

 Create a speech, and share it with your stuffed animal crowd like Moses shared with the Israelites.

▶ Think about a story that you want to share. It could be something that happened to you recently, a favorite book of yours, or a story that you recently heard.

> **You'll Need**
> • paper
> • crayons
> • stuffed animals
> • a couch cushion

▶ Practice what you want to share by remembering the beginning, middle, and end of your story.

▶ On a piece of paper, draw three boxes—one each for the beginning, the middle, and the end of your story. Draw a picture of each of the three moments of your story, creating a storyboard of your speech.

▶ Once you are ready, set up your stuffed animals to pretend they are the crowd of Israelites ready to listen to you.

▶ Stand on top of the couch cushion, imagining it is a big rock.

▶ Hold the storyboard speech you created, and use it to tell your story.

> **Why is it important to remember where we've been and what we've learned?**

▶ Just like Moses, share your speech and what you want the crowd to learn from it. How can you use your voice and your body when you share your speech to make sure everyone hears and understands you?

Play Remember the Israelites' journey through the wilderness, and see how quickly you can navigate it.

▶ Decide a starting point and end point for your obstacle course.

▶ Set up the following stations representing different moments from the journey through the wilderness. You may remember these episodes from our previous activities:

> **You'll Need**
> - 2 bedsheets
> - pillows
> - blankets
> - 2 pieces of paper
> - blocks
> - a spray bottle of water
> - ice cream
> - honey

- Cross the Sea of Reeds: Arrange the two bedsheets on the floor to create an alley pathway in between to cross through.

- Climb Mount Sinai: Use pillows and blankets to make a small mountain. Put the two pieces of paper on top of the mountain (to represent the Ten Commandment tablets).

- Build the Menorah for the Tabernacle: Put the blocks in a pile to use to create a miniature Menorah for the Tabernacle.

- Scout out the land: Run to a hiding spot and use your hands as binoculars (or the ones you made in chapter 37), pretending that you are scouting out the land with the spies.

- Hit the rock to get water: Put the spray bottle on the floor to be the rock that springs water.

- Reach the "Land of Milk and Honey": At the final station, prepare ice cream with honey on it to represent the land of Canaan.

▶ On the count of three, start your obstacle course while the other person sets a timer. See how quickly you can navigate your way through the course, completing each station: cross through the Sea of Reeds, climb Mount Sinai and get the Ten Commandments, build a miniature Menorah, hide and scout out the land, "hit" the rock and spray water on yourself, take a bite of "milk and honey" in Canaan.

> What do you want to remember about being a kid when you are a grown-up?

CHAPTER 45

One in the World

Deuteronomy 3:23–7:11 • *Parashat Va'etchanan* • וָאֶתְחַנַּן

Explore the idea of oneness in the world, and create your own mezuzah.

Can you think of things that are unique in the universe—a thing that exists all by itself as the only one of its kind?

"Listen to these important words, everyone," Moses said as he continued his speech from on top of a hill, near the Jordan River at the edge of the land of Canaan. "You need to be prepared for the land flowing with milk and honey!"

Moses shared all of the things that the Israelites would need to do once they arrived in their new home in Canaan. Then he taught the Israelites the words that would become one of the most important prayers for the Israelites—the words of the Sh'ma: "Hear this Israel—God is our only God, and God is one."

"We believe that there is only one God in the universe, who fills every space and brings life to all living things. When we feel small in the great big world, God can help make us feel connected. That is one of the things that makes us unique as a people," Moses said.

The Israelites looked up at the stars and thought about the oneness of God in the vast universe. They remembered all of the ways that God helped them on their journey, and they felt a feeling of wonder and awe.

"Teach these words to your children," Moses told the people. "Say the words when you are home and when you are away, when you get up in the morning and when you go to sleep. When you arrive in Canaan, write these special words on your doorposts. This way, these words will always be with you as you come and go."

Imagine Imagine decorating your doorposts as the Israelites did to remember the words from the Torah.

▶ Why do you think the Israelites needed the Sh'ma prayer written on their doorposts? How do you think you would feel every time you saw the words on your doorpost?

▶ Once they set up their homes in Canaan, how else might the Israelites remember all the ways that God helped them in their journey?

> In what ways are you the same as other people? In what ways are you different?

Make Design and decorate a mezuzah for your doorpost.

▶ Jewish tradition interprets "write these words on your doorposts" to mean the small box with words inside that we now call a mezuzah. Make a creative version of your own mezuzah.

▶ Design the paper that goes inside the box. What makes you feel awe and wonder in the world? (It might be something found in nature, a big building, or the night sky.) On a piece of construction paper, draw a picture of all the things that make you say "Wow" in the world.

▶ If you'd like, you can draw or trace the word *sh'ma* in Hebrew. It means "listen," and it looks like this: שמע.

▶ Use markers, crayons, stickers, and any other craft materials you want to decorate the outside of the cardboard tube.

▶ Once you are done, roll up your "Wow" picture and insert it inside the cardboard tube.

▶ Using tape, hang your mezuzah up on a doorpost of your favorite room, on a diagonal, with the top closer to the inside of the room. Every time you enter this room, think about the drawing you made and how it makes you feel safe and feel awe.

You'll Need
- small cardboard tube
- construction paper
- markers
- crayons
- stickers
- tape

Play **Play this game to think about the concept of oneness in the world.**

> The Sh'ma prayer is about the idea that there is only one God.

> Are there any objects that you have only one of in your home? What other objects exist as only one in the world around you (for example, the moon)?

> How do the decorations, pictures, and art that you hang up in your house or your school help you remember things? How do they make you feel?

> Go on a scavenger hunt around your house or classroom and through your neighborhood to find objects that are singular (meaning that there is only one of them). If there's more than one of the item in your house or school, it doesn't count.

> How do you celebrate the things that make you unique?

> Write a list or draw a picture of all of the one-of-a-kind things you find on your hunt. What is special about being unique?

CHAPTER 46

Tasting the Land

Deuteronomy 7:12–11:25 • *Parashat Eikev* • עֵקֶב

Explore the sights, smells, and tastes of the "seven kinds" of food in the land of Canaan.

Have you ever tasted a new food when visiting a new place?

"I bet you are ready for new kinds of food after all this time in the wilderness," Moses said to the Israelites. "You'll find lots of new treats in the land of Canaan—a whole bunch of foods that grow there in your new home!"

The Israelites couldn't help feeling really excited. Their eyes got wide, and their bellies started rumbling. After eating manna for so long in the wilderness, the Israelites were very ready for some new smells and tastes to fill them up.

"God brought you to a beautiful new home," Moses told them. "It is a land flowing with milk and honey."

He told them Canaan was a place filled with streams, and springs, and fountains. It was a place where many things could grow and thrive. Moses said, "When you arrive, be on the lookout for seven special kinds of food that grow there: wheat, olives, barley, dates, pomegranates, figs, and grapes."

Moses told them that they would be able to eat and eat, and there would be enough food for everyone. The Israelites closed their eyes as he spoke, and their mouths watered—they couldn't wait to taste these new foods and explore the land.

Imagine — **Answer these questions as you imagine the Israelites experiencing new tastes in Canaan.**

▶ Manna just appeared for the people to eat in the wilderness, but they needed to grow their own food in Canaan. If you were an Israelite, how would you feel about this change?

▶ Which of the seven foods would you be most excited to try when you arrived in the land?

> Have you ever eaten a fruit or vegetable that you picked from a garden? How did it taste?

 Make — Create a "Seven Kinds" Tasting Menu from the special foods the Israelites will find in the land of Canaan.

▶ Go shopping for the following items together: wheat (crackers), barley (you can get barley cereal), dates, pomegranate (seeds), figs, grapes, and olives.

▶ Lay them out in a row, and prepare them to eat.

▶ Take a taste of each item. Close your eyes while you taste, so that you can really focus on the flavor of each one.

You'll Need
• wheat (crackers)
• barley (cereal)
• dates
• pomegranate (seeds)
• figs
• grapes
• olives

▶ Rate each of the seven kinds of food, and decide on your favorite.

> What types of fruits and vegetables grow where you live?

▶ Why do you think these seven foods are the most important in the new land? What could the Israelites make with these seven ingredients?

Play Think of your favorite foods, and play a guessing game with each other to imagine tasting them.

▶ Imagine spending lots of time in the wilderness without your favorite foods. Think of a few foods that you would really miss.

▶ Once you come up with a few ideas, try to get someone else to guess the food you are dreaming of.

> What kinds of flavors are your favorite? What kinds of flavors are your least favorite?

▶ One person closes their eyes. The other person gives three clues about the food they are thinking of, without saying the name of the food (for example: It is round, it is red, and it is a fruit). The other person tries to guess the food by imagining tasting it with their eyes closed (It's an apple).

▶ Now switch, so that everyone has a chance to come up with the clues and to guess. How many dream foods can you guess?

> Are there any foods you used to dislike but now like? What changed?

CHAPTER 47

Time for the Temple

Deuteronomy 11:26–16:17 • *Parashat R'eih* • רְאֵה

**Design the Holy Temple, and count out a tenth of
your food to bring as a thank-you gift.**

Have you ever given someone a gift to say thank you?

"When we get to Canaan, we're going to build permanent houses instead of our portable tents, right Moses?" asked a *kohein*, a priest who worked in the portable temple called the Tabernacle.

"Yes, that's right," Moses told him.

"So what's going to happen to the Tabernacle when we get to Canaan? Will we set it up there?" asked the *kohein*.

"The same is true with the Tabernacle," Moses answered the *kohein* as he continued his speech to the people from on top of the hill at the border of the land of Canaan. "Now that you will finally be building a home, God wants you to take down the Tabernacle and build something more permanent."

Once in Canaan, the people would build the first Holy Temple—a more permanent space for them to gather, celebrate, and give thanks. "We'll need everyone's help to build the new Temple. It will be a place where we can show our thanks to God," Moses said.

"How can we show our thanks?" asked the *kohein*.

"You'll bring gifts to the Temple, just like you brought gifts to the Tabernacle," Moses said.

Moses explained that everyone across the land would bring one-tenth of all the food they grow to the Temple, as a gift to show thanks. The *kohein* and the rest of the Israelites imagined all of the vegetables and fruits growing across the land of Canaan, sprouting out of the ground and falling off the trees. They couldn't wait to package them up as presents for the Temple.

Imagine Imagine yourself building the Temple when you arrive in the land of Canaan.

▶ Why do you think it was important for the Israelites to build a permanent Temple in the land of Canaan?

▶ What fruits and other foods would you want to bring to the Temple as a thank-you gift?

> What is the most interesting or special building you've ever visited? What made it so memorable?

 Make Design and build your own version of the Holy Temple.

▶ Look at the image of what the Temple looked like in Canaan. What different components do you see?

You'll Need
• building supplies (plastic building bricks, magnetic tiles, blocks)

▶ Collect building supplies of your choice.

▶ Using the materials, construct your own version of the Holy Temple.

▶ How can you build a strong structure that doesn't easily fall down? Experiment with different ways to stack and build your materials to create the sturdiest building you can.

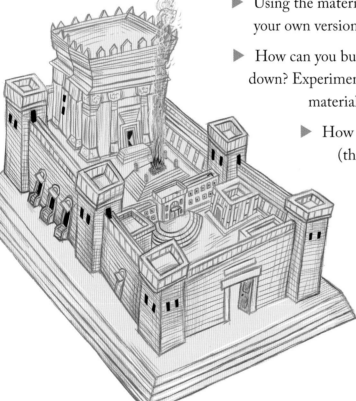

▶ How is your Temple different from the Tabernacle (the temporary temple that was built to be transported in the desert) you built earlier in your adventures? How is it similar?

> Have you ever slept in a temporary structure, like a tent? What makes a tent different from a permanent house?

Explore

Give one-tenth of your food to the Temple.

▶ Fill a few small bowls each with a pile of small foods (cereal, pretzels, etc.).

▶ Think about how the Israelites would give one-tenth (one out of every ten pieces) of the food they grew as a gift.

▶ Start with one of the piles. Count out nine pieces. Put the tenth piece aside in a dedicated bowl for the Temple.

▶ Keep counting, separating every tenth piece into the dedicated bowl.

▶ Once you've separated one-tenth of the food for the Temple, put it in a box or a container that you can decorate. Create a gift box for your present to the Temple.

> **You'll Need**
> - small bowls
> - cereal
> - pretzels
> - box or container
> - Holy Temple (from the MAKE activity)

> Have you ever given a gift to someone to say thank you? What did you give?

▶ Now, holding your gift box, walk across the room toward the Temple you built. Imagine that you are traveling from your home in Canaan to the Temple.

▶ Deliver your gift to the miniature Temple you built, and put it inside. What does it feel like to give this gift?

▶ Enjoy a snack from the portion that you kept.

CHAPTER 48

You Be the Judge

Deuteronomy 16:18–21:9 • *Parashat Shof'tim* • שׁוֹפְטִים

Take on the role of the judge, and decide what you think is fair.

Who helps you learn important rules and reminds you how to follow them?

"Moses, once we are spread out across the land of Canaan, who will help us solve problems when we disagree?" the Israelites asked.

They thought about all of the times they fought and complained in the wilderness along the way. They would definitely need some help.

"When you get to Canaan, choose a group of people to be in charge of making sure everyone follows the rules. That will be really important as you build your new neighborhoods together," Moses told the people, as he continued his speech from on top of a hill at the border of the Jordan River.

"Make sure that each part of the land has someone to be a judge, just as we did in our campsite here in the wilderness," he told them. "The judges will help decide what is right and remind everyone of the lessons we learned in the wilderness. They'll use these rules to help you solve problems and disagreements. Justice, justice you shall pursue!"

"What does 'justice' mean?" one Israelite asked.

"'Justice' means 'acting with fairness.' It is your job to make sure that the people treat each other and the land with respect. The rules and lessons that God gave us in the wilderness can be your guide!" said Moses.

Imagine Imagine yourself choosing the judges who would help solve problems in Canaan when people disagreed.

▶ Why do you think it would be important for the Israelites to create a plan to make things fair and safe once they settle in the land?

▶ What type of person do you think the Israelites needed to choose as a judge? What qualities did they need to have?

> Why is it important for everyone to know and agree on a set of rules?

Explore Balance the scales of justice.

▶ This section of the Torah includes the famous quote, "Justice, justice you shall pursue!" This means, "You should always try to be as fair as possible." A common symbol for justice is a balanced scale. Experiment with this symbol for justice by making your own scale.

▶ Punch two holes on opposite sides of the rim of a cup.

▶ Run one piece of string or yarn through the holes of the cup, and tie the string at the top, so that the cup can hang down from the string.

▶ Repeat these steps so that you have two cups with string attached.

▶ Hang each cup from the top of the string from either side of a clothing hanger.

▶ One person can hold the hanger out from the top. The other person can experiment by putting different weighted objects (for example: coins, cotton balls, or small candy) in each of the cups to see which side hangs lower. Try to use the objects to balance the cups so that they hang at the same height.

> **You'll Need**
> • 2 paper or plastic cups
> • a hole puncher
> • 2 equally long pieces of string or yarn
> • a clothing hanger
> • various small items of different weights

> Have you ever felt like a rule was unfair? Why?

Play **Become the judge of your stuffed animals, and decide what you think is fair.**

▶ Arrange the chairs in a triangle so that two of the chairs are facing the third.

▶ Put each of the stuffed animals in a chair, facing you. They will stand in as the Israelites before the judge.

You'll Need
● 3 chairs
● 2 stuffed animals
● a blanket

▶ Wrap a blanket around yourself as your judge's robe, and sit in the chair facing the stuffed animals.

▶ Read aloud the following scenarios, or create your own. For each scenario, make a decision for what you think should happen to the stuffed animal characters:

• A child's parents told her to clean up her toys, but she was having fun and didn't want to stop playing. Her parents asked her three times, and she didn't listen. What should happen now?

• Two children were playing together, and they both reached for the same toy at the same time. They both feel that they deserve to play with the toy first. They won't let go of the toy. What should happen next?

• A parent said he would take his child to the park to play after work, but he's late getting home. By the time he arrives, it is time to eat dinner. What should happen now?

• One child wants to read a scary story, and the other wants to read a funny story. There's only enough time for one bedtime story tonight. What should happen?

How do you think grown-ups decide when to make a rule?

CHAPTER 49

Fence Me In

Deuteronomy 21:10–25:19 • *Parashat Ki Teitzei* • כִּי־תֵצֵא

**Help a lost object find its way back to the owner, and explore
the ways we design a house to keep everyone safe.**

How do you make sure that everyone in your neighborhood is protected?

"You have to think about how you live together in the land of Canaan," Moses told the Israelites. "It's a large, new place, and you'll be spread out. You won't be camping all together anymore. You need to be prepared for all the ways you can take care of each other."

Moses shared many different examples that God taught him, hoping that the people would feel ready to start life in Canaan soon. The Israelites realized they would be building solid houses after living in tents through the wilderness. "What can we do to build our houses in a safe way? How can we keep our neighbors safe?" they asked.

Moses showed them how to design their new neighborhoods when they started to build houses. He said, "You'll put patios on your roofs to enjoy the fresh air. You should build fences around these flat rooftops, so that no one accidentally falls. It is your job to think about how you can protect each other in your new home."

Moses also taught them ways to take care of each other. He said, "If you find a lost object, it means that someone is missing it!"

"What should we do?" they asked.

"You need to do everything you can to return the object to the owner," Moses taught the people.

The Israelites learned another very important lesson: to respect other people, even if they are different from you. "You should think of people from other places, like the Egyptians, as your brothers and sisters," Moses said.

"The Egyptians? After everything that happened there?" the Israelites wondered.

"Yes—remember that before that, the Egyptians gave our ancestors food when they were hungry. They took our people in when we needed help," said Moses.

The Israelites learned that it was important for them to care about everyone, especially people who are different from them.

 **Imagine** Imagine yourself learning about the ways you can keep your Israelite community safe in your new home.

▶ Can you think of other ways the Israelites could keep each other safe in their new home?

▶ Why do you think it would be important for the Israelites to think about ways to build a safe community in the land of Canaan?

▶ What do you think the Israelites could do to find the owner of a lost object? How could they help?

> What do you need in your house or school to keep you safe? Why is it important to consider everyone's needs when designing our community?

 Explore Walk your neighborhood on a Safety-Design Scavenger Hunt to think about all of the ways that we design communities to keep people safe.

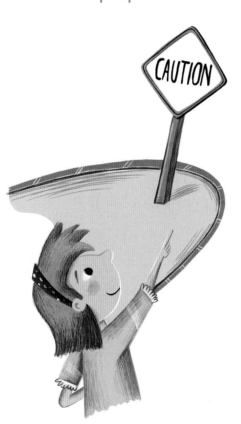

▶ Take a walk in your neighborhood. How do we design our neighborhood to keep people safe?

You'll Need
- paper
- a pen

▶ With this question in mind, explore your community. What features do you notice that are designed to keep people safe (for example, road signs, street lamps, traffic lights, and fire hydrants).

▶ Write or draw all of the objects you see, and try to identify how each one is designed to help keep people safe.

Play Imagine helping return a lost object to its owner.

You'll Need
- stuffed animal
- paper
- crayons
- tape

▶ Pretend that you found a stuffed animal in the road. How would you find its owner? What information would you need? How would you communicate it?

▶ Draw a picture of the stuffed animal. Make it as close to the actual stuffed animal as possible.

▶ Turn your picture into a "Lost Object Found" poster. Think about all of the information that needs to be on the sign for the owner to find you, and add it to your sign.

▶ Make a few copies of your sign, and hang it up around your house or classroom.

▶ One of you can pretend to be the owner, discovering the sign and calling for the stuffed animal, while the other pretends to be the person who found the animal.

▶ Act out the reunion between owner and stuffed animal. The person with the stuffed animal can give it back to the owner.

Think of a time you lost something. Was someone able to return it to you? How did it feel to be reunited with your lost object?

▶ How would the owner feel getting their stuffed animal back? The owner can show how excited they are when they take the stuffed animal in their arms.

▶ Now switch roles so that everyone can play the owner and the returner of the stuffed animal.

CHAPTER 50

Find the
First Fruit

Deuteronomy 26:1–29:8 • *Parashat Ki Tavo* • כִּי-תָבוֹא

**Collect the first fruits from your trees to bring to the Temple,
and build a monument of stones when you arrive in the land.**

How do you set up a new home when you move in?

"It's almost time to enter the land of Canaan, and you are finally ready for it," Moses said to the Israelites. They had wandered for forty years through the desert, seeing all of the amazing things that God did to help them along the way. But today felt different. The Israelites could finally see, hear, and understand how amazing it was that they were freed from Egypt and made their way across a huge wilderness to reach the land that was promised to their ancestors so many years before.

"When you arrive in Canaan, gather a bunch of large stones," Moses told the Israelites as he continued his speech from on top of the hill, at the border of the land. "Write all the lessons you've learned on them."

"What should we do with these large stones after we write everything on them?" the people asked.

"Stack them tall. Make sure you put the stones where everyone can see them, so the people read them and never forget," said Moses, explaining that this sculpture would be a sign of all the things the Israelites had learned together since they camped at Mount Sinai.

Moses also gave them instructions on giving an important gift. "Once you build the city where the Temple will stand, you can bring a gift to the new Temple each year," Moses told the people.

The Israelites would watch for the first fruits to grow on their trees each year. Once the fruits were ready, they would collect these first fruits and bring them as a gift to the Temple. Each year, they would gather together in the middle of Canaan, bringing this bundle of fruit with them.

 **Imagine** Imagine yourself setting up your new home in Canaan, making the stone sculpture, and collecting your first fruits to bring as a gift.

▶ What stories or lessons from the Israelite journey would you want to draw or write on the stone sculpture so that everyone would remember?

▶ Why do you think it was important for Moses to give the Israelites ways to remember everything they had learned? What other things could they do to remember all of the lessons he taught them?

▶ How do you think you would feel bringing the first fruits you grew in the land as a gift to the Temple?

> How can you be a part of making your community strong and beautiful?

 **Make** Create your own stone monument as a symbol of the community you hope to build in the land of Canaan.

▶ Take a walk in your neighborhood. Collect five medium-sized rocks that are flat enough to stack on top of one another.

▶ Think of five values or qualities you think a group of people need to have when working or playing together (for example, kindness or trust).

▶ On each of the rocks, write or draw one value. Paint and design your rocks to reflect these different values or qualities.

▶ Once you are done painting, arrange the rocks in a sculpture. Display your sculpture somewhere others will be able to admire it.

You'll Need
- rocks
- paint
- paintbrushes
- painting clothes or smock (to get messy)

Play Collect the first fruits that grow on your trees to bring to the Temple.

> **You'll Need**
> • multicolored sticky notes
> • markers
> • a plastic bowl

▶ Draw and color the shapes of fruits on multicolored sticky notes. Make sure you have at least four different kinds of fruits represented.

▶ Decide who will be the fruit tree and who will be the Israelite farmer.

▶ Stick the drawings of the fruit to the arms and body of the person who is playing the fruit tree.

▶ You can pretend that a wind blows and shakes the first fruits from the branches of the tree.

What are the ways that you can give back and contribute to your community to help where help is needed?

▶ As the fruits fall to the ground, the Israelite farmer can collect them, sort them, and put them in the plastic bowl to bring to the Temple.

▶ Switch so that everyone has a chance to play both roles.

For Groups:

With multiple players, you can have half the group play the fruit trees while the other half acts as the Israelite farmers. Create an orchard of trees across the room.

CHAPTER 51

It's Your Choice

Deuteronomy 29:9–30:20 • *Parashat Nitzavim* • נִצָּבִים

Prepare to build your new home in Canaan together, and explore the freedom of choice you have to decide how to act.

How do you feel when you get to make your own choice?

"It's time to wake up. Moses has an important message to share with us today!" Two Israelite children opened their eyes from sleep inside their tent. For weeks, they had listened to Moses as he shared stories and lessons with them before they made the big journey into Canaan.

"Is it almost time to pack up and leave?" the children asked their parents.

"Almost," they answered. "We have to make sure we learn as much as we can before we go."

As the sun rose over the camp, the Israelites gathered to listen and learn at the foot of the hill where Moses stood. The children looked up at the crowd—everyone was there.

"You stand here today, all of you—the youngest to the oldest, the leaders, the families—together, as one people, ready to make a home in the land of Canaan," Moses said.

"If you follow all of the lessons that I've taught you, you will find happiness in the land of Canaan," he told them. "You have the power to choose what happens."

"It's up to us?" the children asked.

"Everyone is given the choice to make their own decisions on how to live their lives," Moses said. "Now that you have learned everything that God gave me to teach you, what happens next is up to you."

"When we build our new home in Canaan, we hope we can remember all of these lessons we learned to know how to do what's right," the children thought.

They closed their eyes and tried to hold on tight to everything they had learned.

Imagine Imagine yourself listening and learning the last lessons from Moses at the campsite before preparing to enter the land of Canaan.

▶ How do you think Moses felt seeing all of the people gathered in front of him to learn, from the youngest Israelite to the oldest Israelite?

▶ What would you have done to remember all of the important lessons that Moses taught the Israelites?

▶ How do you think the Israelites felt knowing that they had the power to choose what to do and how to live once they arrived in Canaan?

> What choices do you get to make every day?

 Make Build a structure together by making choices as a group.

▶ Think about how all of the Israelites gathered to learn from Moses and plan how they would build their home in Canaan together.

▶ Sit at a table with your pile of building materials in front of you.

▶ One at a time, take turns choosing a piece to use in building a structure.

▶ Each person can choose the next piece and add it to the structure.

▶ Work together to build one structure, with each piece adding on to the last person's choice.

> ### You'll Need
> • various building materials, including blocks and plastic building bricks

▶ Once you've used all of the pieces and your structure is complete, talk to each other about what you had in mind when you were building. How did you make decisions together as a group? How did the previous person's ideas inspire your own?

> What do you have to do that you don't get to choose?

Play Play a role-play game to explore the impact of the choices you make.

▶ Visit a playground together. At each of these different locations, act out the following scenarios to explore the choices you can make when playing with someone else. (Alternatively, you can act out these scenarios indoors and pretend to be on the playground. You can also choose to act out the scenarios using toys as the actors.)

▶ One person will act as the choice maker, and the other will play a friend in the scene.

Swings

▶ The choice maker gets on the swing. The friend approaches and asks for a turn on the swing. The choice maker acts out these different options or their own choices. They can:

- Say no and keep swinging without letting the friend have a turn.

- Offer a turn to the friend after three more swings.

- Jump off the swing right away and let the friend swing.

▶ What do you choose?

> What does it mean to make a good choice? How do you know if the choice you are making is a good one?

Slide

▶ The choice maker wants to go down the slide, but their friend is sitting at the top of the slide. The friend says, "I'm scared to go down the slide, and I don't know what to do." The choice maker acts out these different options or their own choices. They can:

- Ignore the friend and slide down anyway.

- Tell the friend to slide down right behind them and go down slowly together.

- Offer to leave the slide and play something else with the friend.

▶ What do you choose?

Jungle Gym

▶ The choice maker wants to play superheroes on the jungle gym, but the friend wants to play pirates. The choice maker acts out these different options or their own choices. They can:

- Tell their friend that either they play superheroes or they won't play at all.

- Offer to play superheroes first and then pirates.

- Try to make a game with both superheroes and pirates together.

▶ What do you choose?

CHAPTER 52

Lead Us to the Land

Deuteronomy 31:1–30 • *Parashat Vayeilech* • וַיֵּלֶךְ

Celebrate the appointment of Joshua as the next leader of the Israelites, and put the first Torah scroll in the Ark.

How do you know when it is time to let someone else have a turn to be the leader?

After many adventures, Moses had become very old. It was time for a new leader to take the people on the next chapter of their journey. God told Moses to pass on the role of leader to Joshua, who would take the people across the Jordan River and into the land of Canaan.

The big day had finally come. As he woke up and looked out of his tent, Joshua was feeling nervous. He felt butterflies in the pit of his stomach as he watched the Israelites packing up their tents to prepare for the big journey into Canaan.

"Can I really do this? Am I ready to be the leader of the Israelites?" he thought to himself. "After all, Moses led us out of Egypt and through the wilderness all these years. He's the only leader we've ever known!"

Moses looked into Joshua's eyes and said, "You can do this, Joshua. I believe in you," Moses said. "You've got what it takes to lead the people on this next big adventure."

Joshua started to feel less nervous and more excited to take this big step. "Moses, what else do I need to know?" he asked.

As a last gift to Joshua and all of the Israelites, Moses finished writing down the very long Torah scroll—all of their stories, adventures, and lessons that God gave them.

"Keep this Torah safe, and bring it with you into your new home," Moses told Joshua. Moses rolled up the scroll and gave it to Joshua for safekeeping.

Imagine yourself as Joshua, becoming the next leader of the Israelites.

▶ How do you think Joshua felt about becoming the new leader of the Israelites? What do you think he was nervous about? What part of the job do you think made him feel excited?

▶ How would you feel if it was your job to lead the people into the land of Canaan?

> Think about a time that you had the responsibility of leading a group. How did you feel as the leader?

Act out the moment when Moses makes Joshua the new leader of the Israelites.

▶ Write or draw the qualities you think a good leader should have. If the child is too young to write, a grown-up can write down their ideas for them. Decide on three words that describe a leader (for example, kind, patient, and fair). Practice saying these three words out loud.

You'll Need
- paper
- crayons or markers

▶ Decide who will be Moses and who will be Joshua.

▶ Moses can put two hands on Joshua's head.

▶ Act out a ceremony to make Joshua the new leader, using the three words you chose. Using the leadership qualities you wrote down, Moses can say, "Joshua, may you be _____, _____, and _____."

▶ What else might happen at this ceremony? Act out the ideas you invent.

▶ Switch so that everyone has a chance to be blessed and give the blessing of new leadership.

Play **Become a Torah scroll, and enter the Ark for safekeeping.**

▶ Many Jewish communities today have Torahs written on long pieces of parchment, rolled up into a scroll, and kept inside a closet called an Ark. Become the Torah using your body and imagination.

▶ Stretch your body out, and pretend to be a very long piece of parchment.

▶ Without actually touching, one person can pretend to write the Torah on the "parchment" (the other person).

▶ The "parchment" pretends to be the Torah scroll being rolled up by twirling a few times in one direction and then a few times in the other direction.

▶ Wrap a blanket snugly around the "Torah" as the cover around the scroll.

▶ Parade the "Torah" around the room, and lead it to a closet or door. Put the "Torah" inside and use the closet door to pretend to close the Ark. You can also hang a bedsheet between two chairs to be the opening of the Ark.

> Think of a story you have read over and over. Why do you read it again and again? What changes as you read the story again?

CHAPTER 53

A Song to Say Goodbye

Deuteronomy 32:1–52 • *Parashat Ha'azinu* • הַאֲזִינוּ

Write a song for the Israelites, and sing to them as they move toward the land of Canaan.

How can music help us share our feelings in a way that words can't?

"Let me sing to you to say goodbye," Moses said to the Israelites.

It was Moses's last day as leader of the people. He was too old to make the journey ahead, and he would say goodbye to the people before they entered the land of Canaan. He had led them all the way to the edge, but they needed to take the next steps on their own. "As you leave, I want to show you how I feel by sharing a song," Moses told them.

The Israelites gathered all together in the moonlight, huddled up close under blankets—the families with all of their children, the leaders and their tribes, the animals big and small. They all snuggled up close, ready to listen to Moses and his final song. The stars twinkled in the sky above as Moses climbed to the top of the hill one more time.

Moses sang a final prayer to the people, reminding them about all of the places they'd been together and making a wish for their future. He imagined the Israelites building their new home using all of the lessons that he'd taught them. His voice echoed across the hill where they stood, at the spot between the wilderness and the land of Canaan. The Israelites closed their eyes and listened to every word.

 **Imagine** **Imagine yourself saying goodbye to the people by singing them a song.**

▶ How do you think Moses felt saying goodbye to the Israelites before they entered the land of Canaan?

▶ Why do you think he chose to sing a song to the people on his last day with them? How would you choose to say a big goodbye to the Israelites?

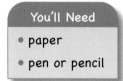

What are the different types of songs you sing on special occasions?

 **Make** **Write a song to commemorate the journey through the wilderness, and perform it for the Israelites as part of their send-off.**

▶ Brainstorm and write down a list of events you can remember from the Israelites' journey through the wilderness, from Egypt to right outside of Canaan.

You'll Need
- paper
- pen or pencil

▶ Choose a melody. You can make up your own, or use a familiar melody that everyone knows. You could use "Twinkle, Twinkle, Little Star" or "Mary Had a Little Lamb."

▶ Use the list you brainstormed and the melody you've chosen, and start thinking about how to bring all of the pieces together to create a song.

▶ You can also create new verses using the structure of "Old MacDonald Had a Farm," reimagined as "Mo-Mo-Moses Took a Trip." See sample lyrics on the next page, and create your own using the list of events you brainstormed. You can create hand movements for each of the actions in the verses and act them out as you perform the song.

Mo-Mo-Moses took a trip, Ee i ee i o.
And on this trip he crossed the sea, Ee i ee i o.
With a splash splash here, and a splash splash there,
Here a splash, there a splash, everywhere a splash splash.
Mo-Mo-Moses took a trip, Ee i ee i o.

And on this trip he climbed Sinai, Ee i ee i o.
With a climb climb here, and a climb climb there,
Here a climb, there a climb, everywhere a climb climb.
Mo-Mo-Moses took a trip, Ee i ee i o.

And on this trip his people whined, Ee i ee i o.
With a whine whine here, and a whine whine there,
Here a whine, there a whine, everywhere a whine whine.
Mo-Mo-Moses took a trip, Ee i ee i o.

Play — Perform your song for the people.

▶ Gather your instruments, and practice your song.

▶ Set up a special spot to perform your song. Arrange your stuffed animals to pretend they are the crowd of Israelites ready to listen to you.

▶ Stand on top of the couch cushion, imagining it is a big rock.

▶ Just like Moses, perform your song for the people, with lots of feeling.

You'll Need
- your song
- instruments
- stuffed animals
- a couch cushion

Why do you think you sometimes choose to sing to mark a special occasion (like a birthday) rather than just talking? How does singing make you feel differently about the occasion?

CHAPTER 54

A New Beginning

Deuteronomy 33:1–34:12 • *Parashat V'zot Hab'rachah* • וְזֹאת הַבְּרָכָה

Climb Mount Nebo, and imagine the Israelites crossing the Jordan River into the land of Canaan.

How do you feel when you start a new adventure?

On his last day as the leader of the Israelites, Moses gathered the people to give them one more blessing. "I want to say goodbye to each tribe one at a time and give you my words of blessing before I go." Moses shared his wish with each tribe, just like Jacob did with each of his children so many years before.

Then Moses climbed to the top of Mount Nebo and saw the land of Canaan stretched out in front of him. "Wow, look at that," Moses said to himself. "It's everything I hoped it would be. My people are home."

He took a deep breath, tried to take in everything he saw, and closed his eyes to remember how beautiful it looked.

"Let's go, everyone! We've got a long day of walking ahead of us," Joshua said to the Israelites.

It was finally time to enter the land of Canaan and start a new chapter of their story, building a home of their own together.

The Israelites packed up their things and took down their tents for the last time as they prepared for their big journey across the Jordan River. The journey through the wilderness had come to an end, but the adventures of the Israelites were only just beginning.

 **Imagine** **Imagine yourself at the end of the journey through the wilderness, getting ready for the adventure into the land of Canaan.**

▶ How do you think the land of Canaan looked from the top of the mountain? What sights do you imagine seeing from way up there?

▶ How do you think you would feel when your feet touched the water of the Jordan River and you were finally about to cross into the land of Canaan, which you had dreamed of for so long?

> How do things look different when you see them from way up high instead of on the ground in front of you?

 Make **Draw the view of the Land of Milk and Honey from the top of Mount Nebo.**

▶ Close your eyes, and imagine Moses walking up Mount Nebo. When he gets to the top, he sees the land of Canaan for the first time. What do you think he sees?

▶ Imagine the mountains, the sand, the rivers, the fruits, the flowers, the trees, and the setting sun.

▶ Open your eyes. Draw a picture of what you imagined when your eyes were closed. Create a beautiful picture of the Land of Canaan from the top of the mountain. Alternatively, build the picture using materials and toys you can find around the house or classroom.

You'll Need
- paper
- crayons
- markers
- building materials and small toys

> Which moments of your adventures through the whole story of the Bible stick out in your memory? What about those moments were so memorable?

Play Bring the final moments of the journey to life on the playground.

▶ Go to your favorite playground. Find the tallest area of the playground.

▶ Imagine that it is the top of Mount Nebo. Climb up, imagining you are Moses. You are very old, and the trail is steep.

▶ When you get to the top, imagine looking out at the land of Canaan. Use your hands as binoculars (or the ones you made in chapter 37), and imagine the view.

▶ Climb down, and find a wide-open spot on the ground.

▶ Using the sidewalk chalk, draw a line representing the water of the Jordan River.

▶ Imagine you are an Israelite, standing at the edge of the river.

> **You'll Need**
> - sidewalk chalk
> - binoculars from chapter 37

▶ Close your eyes, and think about all of the things that have happened across the whole story of the Torah we have played together, from the creation of the world to this moment.

▶ Open your eyes. Count to three, and jump from one side of the water to the other, imagining that you are crossing the river into Canaan.

> Why do you think Jewish people around the world read these stories every year? What do you think you can learn from retelling them again and again?

Completing Deuteronomy
A Celebration Ritual

You've just finished the book of Deuteronomy, and the end of the whole Torah! You listened to Moses share important last lessons before announcing Joshua as the new leader. You are all packed up and ready to follow Joshua across the Jordan River and into the land of Canaan. Wow! You did it. Before we go, let's mark this milestone together.

Unroll the Scroll

Imagine that you are the big scroll of the Torah. Stand really tall, with your arms at your sides. On the count of three, do *five* giant spins to pretend that you are unrolling the entire Torah scroll. One, two, three, spin!

Shout a Cheer

Say together in Hebrew, English, or both:

"Chazak, chazak, v'nit'chazeik!"

"Be strong, be strong, and we'll be strong together!"

You can say these words together, or come up with your own cheer for Deuteronomy. (For example, "We're ready now to enter the land, we'll cross the river hand in hand!")

Celebrate

Have a party to celebrate everything you've learned and explored. Create a dance move based on your favorite character from the Torah. Jump up and down like you are hopping across the Jordan River. Spin to close the Torah before we start from the beginning again. Plan how you want to mark the moment together, and celebrate your own way!

This quick guide can serve as a reference for the overall story of the Five Books of Moses as they are told in this book.

- The whole universe was created, from light and darkness, oceans and plants, to every living creature.

- Noah and Naamah packed up an ark filled with animals and navigated a really big flood safely aboard with their family. After the rain stopped, a rainbow appeared.

- Abraham and Sarah left home in search of a new land where their family could grow.

- Abraham asked Eliezer to find a partner for Isaac, the son of Abraham and Sarah. Rebecca showed kindness to Eliezer's camels and returned home with him to build a life with Isaac.

- Isaac and Rebecca's sons, Jacob and Esau, were total opposites. After getting into a fight with Esau, Jacob ran away from home. He started a family with sisters Rachel and Leah, and they had thirteen children. Many years later, the brothers were finally reunited and forgave one another.

- Jacob's son Joseph was his favorite of all of his children. Joseph's brothers were jealous and created a plan to send him away from home. Joseph was sent to Egypt, where he married and had two sons, Ephraim and Manasseh. Through his amazing dream-interpreting abilities, he became second-in-command to Pharaoh, the king of Egypt. He saved the kingdom from running out of food and reunited with his brothers.

- Many years later, the children of Jacob grew into a big nation called the Israelites. They were slaves to Pharaoh in Egypt, forced to work hard in the hot sun. Yoheved saved her son Moses by sending him away in a basket on the Nile, and his sister, Miriam, helped keep him safe. Pharaoh's daughter, Batya, raised him in the palace.

- Moses led the Israelites to freedom from Egypt and into the wilderness in search of a place of their own. Moses had married a Midianite named Zipporah, who joined the Israelites on their journey.

- Camped at Mount Sinai, the Israelites received the Ten Commandments and the Torah, helping them learn how to become good people to each other in community.

- The Israelites built a temporary temple in the wilderness called the Tabernacle, and Moses's brother, Aaron, led the people in many rituals as a community.

- Moses led the Israelites through the wilderness for forty years, through many adventures.

- After all that time, Moses passed his leadership to Joshua to lead the people into the land of Canaan to build a home.

Materials You May Need

Here is a list of all of the materials used in the activities in *Let There Be Play*.

HOME GOODS

- Aluminum foil
- Backpack
- Baking sheet
- Bandana/cloth
- Basket
- Bedsheets
- Blankets
- Bowls
- Brown paper bags
- Bucket
- Buttons
- Cardboard tube
- Chairs
- Chopsticks
- Clothing
- Cooking utensils
- Costume clothing
- Cotton balls
- Couch cushions
- Cups (plastic or paper)
- Fabric (soft)
- Flashlights
- Grass seed
- Hanger
- Jars
- Leaves
- Measuring cups
- Mirror
- Napkins
- Newspaper
- Pan or skillet
- Paper towels
- Party decorations
- Pillows
- Plastic bag (sealable)
- Plastic containers
- Plastic forks
- Plastic wrap
- Plates
- Potting soil
- Rocks
- Sandpaper
- Socks
- Spatula
- Sponge
- Spoons
- Spray bottle
- Stapler
- Stick
- Sticky notes
- Straws
- String
- Table
- Tissue box (empty)
- Towel
- Water

TOYS

- Balls
- Building blocks
- Dice
- Magnetic tiles
- Musical instrument
- Plastic building bricks
- Play dough
- Sidewalk chalk
- Stuffed animals
- Toy figures

FOOD

- Barley cereal
- Beans (dry)
- Bread
- Candy
- Candy melts
- Cereal
- Dates
- Figs
- Flour
- Graham crackers
- Grapes
- Honey
- Ice cream
- Ice cubes
- Icing
- Olives
- Oil
- Pomegranate seeds
- Popcorn
- Pretzel rods
- Pretzels (small)
- Spices (various)
- Sprinkles
- Wheat crackers

CRAFT SUPPLIES

- Cardboard
- Crayons
- Dot stickers
- Glue
- Hole puncher
- Markers (permanent)
- Markers (washable)
- Paint
- Paintbrushes
- Paper (various colors of construction paper)
- Pen
- Pipe cleaners
- Popsicle sticks
- Poster paper
- Scissors
- Smock
- Tape
- Tissue paper

Acknowledgments

Many people helped bring this book into the world over the last few years. I am grateful to my personal and professional community for supporting me in my growth as an artist, as a Jewish educator, and as a parent.

Thank you to my family for your unending love and encouragement throughout this journey and always.

David—Thank you for being my biggest champion and strongest advocate. Your rabbinic journey became intertwined with this exploration we had at home, and you provided deep wisdom and direction as I made my way through this project. This book wouldn't exist without your love and fierce belief in me. You are my partner in every adventure.

Elior—I will be forever grateful for the magical year we spent playing and creating the activities in this book. It was a gift watching your imagination grow while you developed a deep connection to the Torah.

Amitai—Thank you for sitting on my lap through so many Zoom calls about this project. I can't wait to play through the Torah with you as you grow, and make new discoveries together.

My parents, Mark and Madye—You gave me the gift of a deep Jewish education while fostering my passion for the performing arts. Your fierce love and never-ending support make all of my endeavors seem possible.

To the incredible team at Behrman House—Thank you to David Behrman and Dena Neusner for believing in my vision and championing this project so that it can reach so many families and schools. Thank you to Maxine Handelman for your wonderful notes and enthusiastic support as a reader on this project and to Debra Corman for contributing your biblical knowledge to the project. A huge thank you to my editor Rabbi Deborah Bodin Cohen, whose thoughtful and insightful feedback pushed me to strengthen this work in immeasurable ways.

I also want to share deep gratitude for the following supporters, advocates, colleagues, and friends:

To Joni Blinderman and the Covenant Foundation team, for your immense support and encouragement in my growth as a Jewish educator.

To Sasha Kopp, for your enthusiastic belief that I had a place in the Jewish early childhood ecosystem. You were a cheerleader for this project when it was a glimmer of an idea.

To Nina Meehan, Saul Kaiserman, and Mark Horowitz, for your invaluable mentorship and friendship as I navigated the development of this project.

To Mara Braunfeld, for seeing a connection and making a generous *shidduch*. I am grateful to have you as a friend and colleague—to brainstorm and dream with you as we both work to bring Torah to families in exciting new ways.

To Rabbi Jethro Berkman and the entire team at the Mandel Institute, for providing me with a transformative learning experience as part of the inaugural Jewish Education Leadership Program.

To Daniel Olson, for inspiring me with your own creative weekly parashah project on TikTok. Your determination to complete the cycle gave me confidence I could do it too.

To Terry Kaye and Gavi Young, for your wise insights, joyful collaboration, and steadfast friendship.

To Edie Demas and the entire teaching artist team at New Victory, for teaching me how to develop curriculum and use imaginative play to spark wonder for kids, parents, and teachers.

To Rabbi Sharon Kleinbaum, Rabbi Yael Rapport, and Congregation Beit Simchat Torah (CBST), for showing me how Judaism can be relevant, accessible, and joyful. Thank you, too, for providing a space to dream and incubate new ideas as I transitioned from the theater world to Jewish education.

Finally, thank you to my community at Congregation Beth Shalom, for providing a welcoming and loving spiritual home for my family and for my work in Chicagoland.

Jonathan Shmidt Chapman is an award-winning artist, writer, and Jewish educator. As the founder of the K'ilu Company, Jonathan reimagines Jewish early childhood engagement through theater and play. His projects have reached thousands of families and classrooms across the country. Jonathan was named the Covenant Foundation's inaugural Jewish Family Education Fellow in 2023. He is also the recipient of a Pomegranate Prize, the Jewish Education Project's Young Pioneers Award, and the Children's Theatre Foundation of America Medallion Award. He was invited to join the inaugural cohort of the Mandel Institute's Jewish Education Leadership Program. Jonathan served as the Producer of Family Programming at Lincoln Center for the Performing Arts in New York City. His theatrical works for children and families have been presented there and at the Kennedy Center and Seattle Children's Theatre, and have been featured by *NBC Nightly News with Lester Holt*, the *New York Times*, and *American Theatre* magazine. Jonathan coauthored *Envisioning the Future of Theater for Young Audiences* for the National Endowment for the Arts, and he currently serves on the faculty at Northwestern University. He holds an MA in educational theatre from New York University. He lives in the Chicago area with his husband, Rabbi David Chapman, and their two children, Elior and Amitai.

Hector Borlasca is an illustrator and graphic designer. His work has appeared in children's books, advertising campaigns, newspapers, textbooks, and more. His children's books include *The Porridge Pot Goblin*, by Jacqueline Jules, and *Yiddish Saves the Day*, by Debbie Levy. He lives in Buenos Aires, Argentina.